W Hour

THE AZRIELI SERIES OF HOLOCAUST SURVIVOR MEMOIRS: PREVIOUSLY PUBLISHED TITLES

W Hour
Arthur Ney

THE AZRIELI FOUNDATION
www.azrielifoundation.org

Cover and book design by Mark Goldstein
Endpaper maps by Martin Gilbert
Maps on pages xxvi and xxvii by François Blanc

LIBRARY AND ARCHIVES CANADA CATALOGUING IN PUBLICATION

Ney, Arthur, 1930–, author
    W Hour/ Arthur Ney.

(The Azrieli series of Holocaust survivor memoirs; 6)
Includes bibliographical references and index.
ISBN 978-1-897470-41-1 (pbk.)

1. Ney, Arthur, 1930–. 2. Holocaust, Jewish (1939–1945) – Poland – Personal narratives. 3. Warsaw (Poland) – History – Uprising, 1944 – Personal narratives, Jewish. 4. Jewish children in the Holocaust – Poland – Biography. 5. Holocaust survivors – Canada – Biography. I. Azrieli Foundation, issuing body II. Title. III. Series: Azrieli series of Holocaust survivor memoirs.; Series VI

DS134.72.N49A3 2014   940.53'18092   C2014-900507-5

The Azrieli Series of Holocaust Survivor Memoirs

Naomi Azrieli, Publisher

Jody Spiegel, Program Director
Arielle Berger, Managing Editor
Farla Klaiman, Editor
Elizabeth Lasserre, Senior Editor, French-Language Editions
Aurélien Bonin, Educational Outreach and Events Coordinator,
    Francophone Canada
Catherine Person, Educational Outreach and Events Coordinator,
    Quebec region
Elin Beaumont, Senior Educational Outreach and Events Coordinator
Tim MacKay, Digital Platform Manager
Eric Bélisle, Digital Communications and Operations Specialist
Susan Roitman, Executive Assistant and Office Manager (Toronto)
Mary Mellas, Executive Assistant and Human Resources (Montreal)

Mark Goldstein, Art Director
François Blanc, Cartographer
Bruno Paradis, Layout, French-language editions

Contents

Series Preface:
In their own words...

In telling these stories, the writers have liberated themselves. For so many years we did not speak about it, even when we became free people living in a free society. Now, when at last we are writing about what happened to us in this dark period of history, knowing that our stories will be read and live on, it is possible for us to feel truly free. These unique historical documents put a face on what was lost, and allow readers to grasp the enormity of what happened to six million Jews – one story at a time.

David J. Azrieli, C.M., C.Q., M.Arch
Holocaust survivor and founder, The Azrieli Foundation

Since the end of World War II, over 30,000 Jewish Holocaust survivors have immigrated to Canada. Who they are, where they came from, what they experienced and how they built new lives for themselves and their families are important parts of our Canadian heritage. The Azrieli Foundation's Holocaust Survivor Memoirs Program was established to preserve and share the memoirs written by those who survived the twentieth-century Nazi genocide of the Jews of Europe and later made their way to Canada. The program is guided by the conviction that each survivor of the Holocaust has a remarkable story to tell, and that such stories play an important role in education about tolerance and diversity.

Millions of individual stories are lost to us forever. By preserving the stories written by survivors and making them widely available to a broad audience, the Azrieli Foundation's Holocaust Survivor Memoirs Program seeks to sustain the memory of all those who perished at the hands of hatred, abetted by indifference and apathy. The personal accounts of those who survived against all odds are as different as the people who wrote them, but all demonstrate the courage, strength, wit and luck that it took to prevail and survive in such terrible adversity. The memoirs are also moving tributes to people – strangers and friends – who risked their lives to help others, and who, through acts of kindness and decency in the darkest of moments, frequently helped the persecuted maintain faith in humanity and courage to endure. These accounts offer inspiration to all, as does the survivors' desire to share their experiences so that new generations can learn from them.

The Holocaust Survivor Memoirs Program collects, archives and publishes these distinctive records and the print editions are available free of charge to libraries, educational institutions and Holocaust-education programs across Canada. They are also available for sale to the general public at bookstores.

The Azrieli Foundation would like to express appreciation to the following people for their invaluable efforts in producing this book: Sherry Dodson (Maracle Press), Sir Martin Gilbert, Andrea Knight, Malcolm Lester, David Ney, and Margie Wolfe and Emma Rodgers of Second Story Press.

About the Glossary

The following memoir contains a number of terms, concepts and historical references that may be unfamiliar to the reader. For information on major organizations; significant historical events and people; geographical locations; religious and cultural terms; and foreign-language words and expressions that will help give context and background to the events described in the text, please see the glossary beginning on page 179.

Introduction

"My family was gone. I was alive but alone in the world, and had to do something to survive. I congratulated myself for having outwitted the Germans and the other antisemites whose paths I had crossed during the occupation, but I knew I had to continue to hide my identity – it was not yet possible to end my double life. I only saw a future for myself as Piotr Grodzieński."

Germany's unconditional surrender to the Allies in May 1945 did not spell an end to Piotr Grodzieński's troubles. The adolescent Grodzieński, a student and resident of a Catholic orphanage in Poland, had guarded a very dangerous secret since 1943. He feared revealing, even to his closest friends, that he was actually – or perhaps more accurately, also – Artur Ney, a sixteen-year-old Jew. He was one of an estimated 5,000-20,000 Jews in the liberated territories in the newly independent Polish state who continued to live under false identities they had assumed during the war.[1]

While confined to the Warsaw ghetto in the early 1940s, Artur Ney's father had providentially purchased for him the baptismal certificate of a boy who had been murdered by the Germans. But the then twelve-year-old Artur, who had developed a knack for smuggling wares in and out of the ghetto, gave no thought to Piotr Grodzieński's document until he found himself caught on the "Aryan" side of the city in April 1943. Unable to return to his family, he watched from the distance as the ghetto's inhabitants rose in a final stand against the Germans rather than face deportation to Treblinka. Alone in the world, he thereafter clung to Grodzieński's identity as his only protection, even a year and a half after the war had ended.

By this time, however, many of the features of his assumed identity were no longer fictive: he had indeed lost his parents, in addition to many others in his large and close-knit family. He had also converted to Catholicism, a decision he justified to himself as necessary to protect his life despite misgivings that such an act – traditionally viewed by Jews as a form of betrayal of both God and the Jewish people – would have dismayed his family. Moreover, he was quite pleased with some aspects of his new identity, such as the Polish non-Jewish friends he had made, the "un-Jewish" skills he had acquired while working for farming families, the responsibilities with which he was entrusted by the priests, and the privilege of attending a humanities high school (*gimnazjum*).

When Artur began writing his memoir in the fall of 1946, Nazi persecution of Jews had ended, a communist-dominated government discouraged public expressions of antisemitism, and surviving Jews in Poland were encouraged by authorities to come out of hiding. He was, nonetheless, acutely aware that anti-Jewish feeling, prevalent throughout Polish society before the war, had if anything become radicalized by the experience of almost six years of brutal German occupation, which had both preached the complete dehumanization and murder of Jews, and criminalized assistance to them. Evidence of this could be found in the hostile and frequently violent behaviour that greeted surviving Jews, often at the hands of their former neighbours, as they returned home. A pogrom that resulted in more than forty Jewish fatalities in the city of Kielce in July 1946 was but the most dramatic illustration of such sentiments.[2] Further, the new pro-Soviet regime, lacking strong support among ethnic Poles, relied heavily on Jews to fill clerical and administrative functions. This only strengthened the existing stereotype linking Jews to communism, providing yet another reason for Artur to conceal his identity. As he reports, many a Pole resented the fact that dealing with civil servants after the war to obtain basic necessities meant "going to them," a reference to Jews who had survived in the USSR and returned as soldiers with the conquering Red Army.

Perpetuating a double identity weighed as heavily upon Artur's conscience as the anxiety of being discovered to be a Jew oppressed him. He began this memoir, a riveting tale of survival, loss and ambivalence, for fear of forgetting family and friends who had perished. He abbreviated names in order to veil them from his peers, whom he did not fully trust. He completed the memoir decades later not in Poland but in the safety of distant Canada, years after coming to some kind of peace with his very complicated feelings toward his native land. Its contents are a testament to the amazing resourcefulness, bravery and luck of his barely adolescent self.

Explicit in its depictions yet devoid of both sentimentalism and graphic detail, Ney's memoir is as much the story of a young man's coming of age under the most dire of circumstances as it is a gripping account of some of the most important events in Poland's history – from both Jewish and Polish perspectives – during World War II. As such, it offers a unique reflection on Jewish-gentile relations in Poland between the two world wars, during the Holocaust and in its immediate aftermath.

Artur Ney, or Turek as he was known affectionately in the Polish diminutive, was born into an aspiring middle-class Jewish family, the owners of Poland's first dry cleaning plant, in 1920s Warsaw. Despite the family's relative affluence and advanced degree of cultural and linguistic Polonization, he lived, as did most Jews, with his extended family in a crowded apartment in the Jewish section of the city. While residing in the ethnic Polish section of the city was conceivable, he notes, it was an option available only to those with enough wealth and willingness to tolerate a certain amount of discrimination in a society that was both highly stratified and clearly delineated along ethnic lines. Thus, in Ney's words, when the war erupted in September 1939, "It was easy for the Germans to divide and conquer – the Jewish population and the Polish majority had little positive contact and did not trust each other."

Since the late medieval period, Jews had concentrated in large numbers on the territory of the erstwhile Polish-Lithuanian Commonwealth, an enormous, multi-ethnic state that ceased to exist when neighbouring empires – Prussia, Austria and Russia – divided and swallowed up its territory at the end of the eighteenth century. When Poland was reconstituted as an independent state after World War I, Jews – alongside chiefly Ukrainians, Belorussians, Lithuanians and Germans – belonged to the group of so-called national minorities that made up about a third of the new state's population, especially in its eastern provinces.[3] While most Jews shared the poverty of the Christian peasant majority, they were distinguished not only by religion but by their concentration in urban areas and a way of life that included unique customs, distinctive dress and a pattern of employment characterized mainly by work in commerce, artisanry and light industry. Moreover, most Jews spoke Yiddish as their native language and prayed in Hebrew; in contrast, Catholic Poles employed Polish and Latin for largely the same purposes. In short, the Jewish presence in Poland was both ancient and conspicuous. It was indispensable to the economic development of the country and, in the period between the two world wars, would come to play an increasingly important role in its cultural and political life as well.[4]

Numbering more than 3 million, Jews made up roughly 10 per cent of interwar Poland's overall population. As may be expected of so large a group, Polish Jewry was quite diverse within itself and divided into rival factions competing for leadership in communal and state institutions. Despite the popular stereotype equating Jews with communism and support for the Soviet Union, the vast majority of Jews, who were traditionally religious and small business owners, had little sympathy for Poland's dreaded eastern neighbour and its anti-religious, anti-capitalist ideology. A small minority of Jews voted for general Polish parties, particularly the Polish Socialist Party (PPS), or supported communism (which was then illegal in Poland). Most Jews voted instead in state and city elections for distinctively Jewish parties offering competing visions for their future. The dominant ideologies among Jews of the day were religious Orthodoxy, socialism and nationalism, although these streams often mixed. Nationalism meant programs for cultural autonomy for Jews and other peoples in a multinational Polish state or support for the Zionist vision of creating a Jewish homeland in Palestine, which was under British administration since the end of World War I.

Prior to the interwar period, many Jews knew Polish, perhaps imperfectly, for purposes of commerce and other forms of interaction with non-Jews. But relatively few spoke it as their home language or identified with Polish national and cultural aspirations. Indeed, the stereotypically Jewish manner of speech in Polish, as well as Jewish dress and custom, was the subject of mockery and vaudeville-style comedy.⁵ It was therefore a badge of pride for Artur as a child that he possessed an uncle who lived outside the Jewish quarter in Warsaw, was known by a Polish pseudonym, rode a motorcycle and wore fashionable "European" dress – in essence, escaped expectations of Jews as strange and "unmanly" and thus passed comfortably in Polish Catholic society.

Jews represented as much as one-third of the nearly one million residents of Poland's capital. This made for the largest Jewish community in all of Europe in the interwar period and the second largest in the world, second only to New York City at this time. The percentage of the population that was Jewish in such important cities such as Bialystok, Lodz and Vilna was even higher. This was cause for profound alarm among Polish ethno-nationalists, including high-ranking members of the Catholic clergy, who minced no words to warn the public that the Jews' allegedly overwhelming and baneful influ-

ence on the economy and public life was depriving Poles of rightful
control over their own country and transforming it into a morally
dissolute "Judea." In contrast with views of Slavic minorities, who
were also usually viewed with disfavour but still seen as capable of
being assimilated under the right circumstances, little hope or desire
existed among much of Polish society for Jews to be fully integrated.[6]

While it would be a gross exaggeration to describe all Poles as hostile to Jews and wishing them harm, Jews, as long as they remained
Jews, were widely seen as alien and incompatible with Polish national
character whatever their degree of acculturation and their private
views and loyalties. Even their liberal defenders, usually to be found
in the parties of the Polish Left, generally expected the dissolution of
any vestiges of a distinctively Jewish identity as a condition for their
full acceptance in Polish society. More pronounced negative attitudes
toward them ran the gamut from comic bemusement and suspicion
to traditional religious animosity and modern racial antisemitism.

The reborn Polish state was poor, largely agricultural and very
much wary of its large and powerful neighbours, Germany and the
USSR. It struggled to strike a balance between promoting the interests of its ethnic majority and respecting the rights of its national minorities, which were guaranteed by an international treaty – known
as the Polish Minority Treaty – that the fledgling state had signed under duress in return for Allied recognition at the end of World War I.
National minorities were affected by various forms of discrimination
such as the gerrymandering of electoral districts to support ethnic
Polish interests, the shabby treatment of their representatives in
the parliament, and a lack of government funding (and at times of
harassment) for schools functioning in their languages. Jews faced
severe obstacles to obtaining employment in the civil service and in
gaining admission to institutions of higher learning. Although their
situation improved somewhat once Marshal Piłsudski, seen by Jews
as a benevolent protector against antisemitic forces, seized power in
1926, the basic pattern did not change and pauperization grew. Such

trends only intensified as ethnically exclusivist forms of Polish nationalism, which strove for a uniformly Catholic and Polish country,
took increasing hold as World War II approached. By the latter half
of the 1930s, after the death of Marshal Piłsudski, this resulted in increasing violence against Jews and more systematic attempts, both
official and unofficial, to drive them from the economy and, many
hoped, from the country. In this respect, Poland was, however, hardly
unique as most countries in the region gravitated toward authoritar-
ian and ethnically intolerant regimes in the interwar period. Indeed,
several, including Poland, came to repudiate the National Minorities
Treaty that they had signed after World War I.

On the other hand, the opening of Polish public elementary
schools to Jewish children after World War I helped to effect a radical
shift in Jewish attitudes and conduct as a new generation mastered the
Polish language and came to identify with the state and the cultural
legacy of the Polish lands. Indeed, most Jewish children attended free
state elementary schools rather than any of the private Jewish educational networks – religious or secular – offering primary education
in Yiddish or Hebrew, a language that had ceased to be spoken some
2,000 years ago but was revived for everyday speech by the Zionist
movement. They imbibed the values of romantic Polish culture and
devotion to the state and its symbols. Alongside a tremendously vi-
brant culture – both traditional and modern – that existed in Hebrew
and, above all, Yiddish, Jews and individuals of Jewish origin increasingly became contributors to general Polish culture, producing some
of twentieth-century Poland's finest writers, poets, musicians and
artists. At the same time, they contributed an emerging Jewish culture that was Polish in language but Jewish nationalist or religious in
orientation.[7] Polish-Jewish youth such as Artur Ney were part of a
generation in transition, one undergoing varying degrees of secular-
ization, political activism and language shift. It was thus natural for
Jews – even supporters of Jewish nationalism – to be Polish patriots
despite a feeling of exclusion from larger Polish society.

The invasion of Poland by German forces on September 1, 1939, marked the beginning of World War II. Soviet forces invaded from the east scarcely two weeks later under the pretence of protecting Poland's ethnic Ukrainian and Belorussian citizens, who were kindred populations to the peoples of the Soviet Ukrainian and Belorussian republics, now that the Polish state had collapsed. Poland was thus once again partitioned by its powerful neighbours, this time in accordance with the provisions of a secret pact signed by the Soviet and German foreign ministers Molotov and Ribbentrop the preceding month.[8]

Despite antithetical ideologies, both occupiers treated the local population with great cruelty, ruthlessly eliminating sources of anticipated resistance to its goals through such means as murder, deportations, forced labour and economic restructuring. The Soviet Union, bent on building a socialist empire, emphasized economic class as the relevant factor in identifying its ideological enemies. Nazi ideology, in contrast, was avowedly racist. It called for the subjugation of the peoples in Eastern Europe and the colonization of their territory by ethnic Germans. The former, particularly Slavs such as Poles, Ukrainians and Russians, were seen as inherently inferior and an expendable work force. They could, however, be co-opted in the short run, as circumstances and ideological considerations dictated, for the sake of winning the war and larger plans to create *Lebensraum* ("living space") for the German *Volk*. To Jews, however, Nazi policy was unambiguous. The Soviets deported and sometimes murdered Jews who refused to cooperate with them or were ideologically objectionable. But they also entrusted those deemed reliable and useful with positions of authority, either because they possessed pro-Soviet attitudes or the fear of Hitler and his accomplices guaranteed their loyalty. Such treatment only served to confirm in the minds of antisemites that Jews were collectively behind hated communist regimes and guilty of abetting the Soviets. These views were strengthened by German propaganda aimed at civilian populations, particularly after

Germany invaded the U S S R in the summer of 1941 and rapidly seized much of its territory, including the Soviet zone of Poland.

Barely an adolescent, Artur was confined, together with his family, to the Warsaw ghetto in late 1940. He managed to survive the wretched conditions of the ghetto as others succumbed to the starvation, filth and disease and to evade deportation to almost certain death thanks to good fortune and the resourcefulness of his relatives. Growing up in the ghetto, where the rules of polite society no longer prevailed, taught him how to survive in desperate circumstances. Posing as a Catholic orphan during the last two years of the war, he managed to avoid detection despite a number of close calls including a medical examination that revealed that he was circumcised – what would have amounted to a death sentence had the doctor not taken pity on him. It was an asset for survival in Nazi-occupied Poland that Artur spoke Polish free of a Yiddish accent. Of course, in order to pass successfully as a Pole in the Aryan section of Warsaw and beyond, he also needed to master a number of Catholic prayers and ritual greetings, especially those used in rural areas, and to acquire skills, such as tending to animals and lighting a fire, unfamiliar to most Jews as urban denizens.

Despite the distance between Catholic and Jewish societies, Artur depended on the benevolence and assistance of numerous Poles for his very survival as a smuggler in the Warsaw ghetto and, later, while living on the Aryan side of Warsaw and in the Polish countryside. His experiences revealed to him the best and worst in human character, regardless of whether one was a Jew, a Pole or a German. His memoir describes the rapid breakdown of social norms and growing demoralization in the ghetto as desperation seized hold of its population. It also tells, however, of the remarkable ingenuity and bravery of ghetto dwellers who struggled to stay alive and, later, to fight the Germans. His encounters with Poles included both *szmalcowniki*, who extorted money from hidden Jews or denounced them to the Germans for a profit, and people of all walks of life, among them Catholic priests, who risked their lives to keep his secret safe and prepare him for survival.

Motivated by a combination of patriotism and the desire for revenge, he volunteered for the AK (Armia Krajowa), the pro-Western Polish Home Army loyal to the Polish government-in-exile in London. He served during the ill-fated Warsaw Uprising in August-September 1944, when the city's population rose in arms against their occupiers in anticipation of an Allied attack that would strike a decisive blow against the Germans. That Artur encountered expressions of antisemitism among some fellow soldiers, who imitated stereotypical Jewish speech in his presence, did not cool his ardour for the cause. His admiration for his commander is evident. But Allied aid was inadequate and the Soviets, reluctant to aid the Polish resistance, delayed their entry into Warsaw. This allowed the Germans to crush the Uprising and to level the city, effectively undermining Polish opposition to a future pro-Soviet regime once the USSR had definitively routed Germany. Understanding that capture by the Germans meant almost certain discovery of him as a Jew, Artur managed to escape and find shelter outside the city.

The miraculous discovery that Artur's beloved aunt and uncle were still alive, albeit under false identities, helped to seal Artur's decision to re-assert his identity as a Jew and to leave a country toward which he felt so much ambivalence. Without even saying goodbye to friends for fear that the revelation of his Jewish identity would be cause for ill will, he joined his surviving relatives in their pursuit of emigration. In France, where he re-began his life while weighing his options for immigration, the young survivor received an education provided by Zionist organizations active in post-war Europe. He became once again enamoured of a romantic ideal: this time it was the ethos of Jewish self-reliance and the right of the Jewish people to defend itself against hostile parties in its own country. Yet, like so many survivors, he vacillated, as expressed in a popular Yiddish saying of the time, between the desire for *klal yisroel* (the Jewish people as a collective) to establish a homeland in Palestine and for *Reb Yisroel* (Mr. Israel, i.e. the individual Jew) to go to North America.

In the end, he chose Canada, a country in which he already had successful relatives and the chance for a peaceful and prosperous life.

Kalman Weiser
York University
2013

ENDNOTES

1   David Engel, "Poland since 1939," in *The YIVO Encyclopedia of the Jews in Eastern Europe*. New Haven: YIVO and Yale University Press, 2008, vol. 2, 1406. Available online: http://www.yivoencyclopedia.org/article.aspx/Poland/Poland_since_1939

2   On the Kielce pogrom and the subject of anti-Jewish attitudes and violence in Poland immediately after World War II, see Jan Gross, *Fear: Anti-Semitism in Poland after Auschwitz*. New York: Random House Trade Paperbacks, 2007.

3   Norman Davies, "Ethnic Diversity in Twentieth-Century Poland," *Polin* 4 (1989): 143–158.

4   For an excellent survey of Jewish life in interwar Poland, see the now classic work by Ezra Mendelsohn, *The Jews of East Central Europe between the Two World Wars*. Bloomington and Indianapolis: Indiana University Press, 1983, 11–83. For more recent views, see Antony Polonsky's magisterial work, *The Jews in Poland and Russia*. Oxford: Littman Library of Jewish Civilization, 2010, vol. 3. Also, Gershon Bacon, "Poland from 1795 to 1939," in *The YIVO Encyclopedia of the Jews in Eastern Europe*. New Haven: YIVO and Yale University Press, 2008, vol. 2, 1390–1403, available online: *http://www.yivoencyclopedia.org/article.aspx/Poland/Poland_from_1795_to_1939*

5   On Polish attitudes toward Jews, see Alexander Hertz, *The Jews in Polish Culture*. Evanston, IL: Northwestern University Press, 1988. Translated by Richard Lourie; Michael Steinlauf, "Mr. Geldhab and Sambo in 'peyes': images of the Jew on the Polish stage, 1863–1905," *Polin* 4 (1989): 98–128; Alina Cała, "The stereotypes of Jews in Polish eyes and the stereotypes of Poles in the eyes of Jews." *Kwartalnik Historii Żydów* 212 (2004): 528–531.

6 Rogers Brubaker, *Nationalism Reframed. Nationhood and the National Question in the New Europe.* Cambridge: Cambridge University Press, 1996, 100.

7 Chone Shmeruk, "Hebrew-Yiddish-Polish: a Trilingual Culture," in eds. Yisrael Gutman, Ezra Mendelsohn, and Chone Shmeruk. *The Jews of Poland between Two World Wars.* Hanover and London: University Press of New England, 1989, 295–311. Gershon Bacon, "National Revival, Ongoing Acculturation – Jewish Education in Interwar Poland," *Simon Dubnow Institut Jahrbuch* I (2002): 71–92.

8 The literature about Poland during World War II is vast. An excellent recent study is Tim Snyder's *Bloodlands. Europe between Hitler and Stalin.* New York: Basic Books, 2010.

Maps

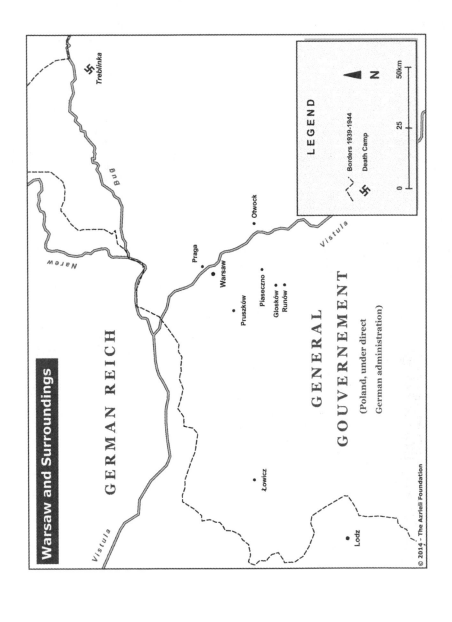

Warsaw and Surroundings

GERMAN REICH

GENERAL
GOUVERNEMENT

(Poland, under direct
German administration)

LEGEND

N

Borders 1939-1944

Death Camp

0   25   50km

Treblinka

Bug

Narew

Vistula

Praga

Warsaw

Otwock

Pruszków

Piaseczno

Głosków

Runów

Vistula

Łowicz

Lodz

Vistula

© 2014 - The Azrieli Foundation

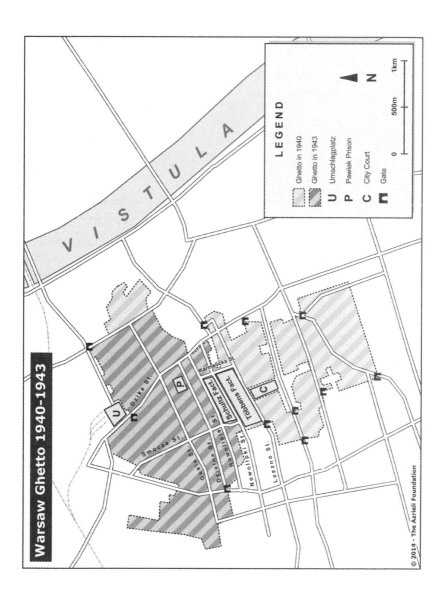

Warsaw Ghetto 1940-1943

VISTULA

LEGEND

- Ghetto in 1940
- Ghetto in 1943
- **U** Umschlagplatz
- **P** Pawiak Prison
- **C** City Court
- ⌐ Gate

N

0   500m   1km

Dzika St.

Smocza St.

Gęsia St.

Dzielna St.

Nowolipie

Nowolipki St.

Leszno St.

Karmelicka St.

Schultz Fact.

Többens Fact.

U

P

C

I would like to dedicate this book first to those of the Polish population during the war who actively sought to stop the genocide in whatever way they could, be that through action or simply through the choice to stay quiet and in doing so risked their lives. Of course those who helped me specifically require mention as you would not be reading this had they been unsuccessful in their collective endeavours.

Second, I would like to recognize my first wife and our marriage that gave me two wonderful sons and allowed me, in a sense, to give something back (at least in a humanist sense) by being a father and working hard to financially support a family with barely a high school diploma to shore up my confidence.

Third, a very special mention needs to be made of the vast efforts of my second wife who, before her very untimely passing, encouraged me to put pen to paper and whose enormous patience served to bring you, dear reader, something that could be proudly published. She took a group of barely inseparable thoughts that I could have never decoded by myself and worked tirelessly to make sense of the jumble of emotions and stories that made up the life of a young adolescent. I had been thrust into such an ever-mounting series of inhuman atrocities that the concept of "future" meant the next morning or even the next ten minutes. I could have never dreamt that I might still be alive today to see these thoughts bring meaning to even one person in this still-tumultuous world in which we live.

Finally I wish to thank my youngest son who, upon the passing of my second wife, took the time and the patience to help me complete this difficult task and without whom the manuscript may have remained a Word document in a number of computers, but would have never seen those essential and final steps that would bring it to publication. L'chaim!

Author's Preface

It has been almost sixty-four years since I wrote the first version of this memoir and I still remember the reasons I began it and the feelings that prompted me to begin.

In the fall of 1946, after an unsuccessful search for my family, I found myself back in Głosków, Poland, at the orphanage run by the Salesian Fathers that I had entered in 1945. Some members of this order had helped me survive in Warsaw after my miraculous escape from the ghetto in 1943. As the oldest of the twenty to thirty boys in the orphanage in Głosków, I was allowed to go to the *gimnazjum* Emilia Plater (an academic high school) located in Zielone, halfway between Warsaw and Głosków.

One grey, windy, late fall afternoon, while doing homework with the other boys in the refectory under the watchful gaze of the Father Superior, who was also reading his breviary, I became conscious of my unhappiness. I was feeling guilty, lonely and frustrated about continuing to hide under my wartime pseudonym, Piotr Grodzieński. Although the war was over and many Jewish people had come out of hiding or returned to Poland, and Jewish organizations were springing up everywhere, I wanted nothing to do with them. I felt quite safe at the orphanage as long as I believed that no one other than the priests knew I was Jewish. I also had the satisfaction of going to high school and meeting other boys (as well as girls!) my own age.

That day, however, I felt that I was not among my own people. My feelings were like those I had experienced during the war: needing to find a way out, the impulse to run away, dissatisfaction with my circumstances and even danger. I had been thinking about the loss of my family more and more often. I was becoming sulky, unsociable, nervous and resentful of the lies I still had to tell because of my false name and identity on the Polish birth certificate my father had bought for me. Daily life was crawling back to normal, and I was furious at myself for being in a situation without a future. It was as if a double threat hung over my head: I knew I didn't want to, and really could not, live forever as Piotr Grodzieński, but I was afraid to unmask myself and start living under my real name.

I had no companion in whom I could confide and unburden my heart. My best friend had been killed in the Holocaust and it was in the sheets of paper on which I began to write my story that I was able to recover my missing friend. Instead of finishing my homework that evening, I remembered the names of my immediate and extended family. I soon found that without realizing what I was doing, I had written the first page of my diary. Being afraid that it would fall into the hands of my classmates, whom I did not fully trust, I wrote down the dates but abbreviated the names. It looked like this:

Bn. 25 VI 1930 in W-w. Fath. Jerzy, m. Pola and Niusia, Arturek-Turek. Liquidation (ghetto) in 1943, 19 IV

Little by little, I began describing the relevant events and the main characters in the story of my life until 1943. It was the fear of forgetting them that led me to write that first version of this memoir.

The Calm Before the Storm

My mother, Pola Ney-Holcman, inherited the first dry cleaning plant in Poland, called Holcman Chemical Cleaning, which my father, Jerzy Ney, administered while she saw to the daily operations. I was born on June 25, 1930, and I recall being a very impressionable and emotional child. I wasn't the best pupil, nor did I have special talents or interests. I didn't know much about sports and my favourite entertainment was playing "cowboys and Indians." I wasn't very tall or well-developed physically, and was sick often. I remember that I liked to gossip and was afraid to sleep in a dark room. My only sibling was my sister, Eugenia, who was five years my senior. We called her Niusia, from Geniusia, a diminutive form of Eugenia. In the same way, I was not called Artur, but Arturek or, usually, Turek.

My paternal grandmother, Henia Ney, came to live with us after the death of her husband around 1935, although she still maintained her own house in Tomaszów Lubelski, a town not too far southeast of Warsaw. My family spent part of our summers there and it later came to symbolize for me the normal, pre-war part of my childhood.

My extended family included Uncle Arthur, my father's brother, his wife, Marysia, and their son, Tolek. My mother's brother, Uncle Kuba, was married to Aneczka, or Anna, and they had two sons – Stach, who was the eldest, and Janek. That part of the Holcman family lived in Lodz, a large industrial city south of Warsaw. Ronia and

Rachela were my father's cousins who, after the death of their mother in the mid-1930s, moved to Warsaw to work in our plant. Ronia became my mother's forelady and Rachela worked as a clerk in the main store on Dzielna Street near our apartment and lived with us.

My father's cousin Rachela was devoted to us body and soul. Because she lived with us and worked relatively short hours, I saw much more of her than of my mother. The sounds of her laughter and singing have stayed in my memory. She always found a reason to laugh and looked at everything from a humorous point of view. She didn't sing very well, yet she knew lots of songs in several languages. I can still sing a Hebrew song she taught me. Rachela didn't have the best life with us, but I was too young to understand this at the time.

Ronia married Józiek a few years before the war, and they were extremely important to me both as a child and much later. Józiek had left home in his early teens when his mother died and his father remarried. He not only looked Polish, he also spoke Polish without a Jewish accent. He didn't speak Yiddish.[1] He was an office manager before the war, living and working among Poles under the name Józef Borzewski. He didn't return to the use of his real name, Borenstein, until after he and Ronia had immigrated to Canada. It made a big impression on me as a young boy to have an uncle who didn't dress like other Jewish people – he wore leather jackets with leather riding boots and breeches. Józiek owned a car and also rode a motorcycle, and my friends were envious whenever he picked me up for a ride. He showered me with pennies and candies whenever I visited. Since they lived in a non-Jewish neighbourhood, these visits ended at the beginning of the German occupation. Ronia and Józiek could not take the chance of their neighbours realizing I was Jewish.

_____

1   For information on Yiddish, as well as on other religious and cultural terms; major
    organizations; significant historical events and people; geographical locations;
    and foreign-language words and expressions contained in the text, please see the
    glossary.

My family lived in the middle of the Jewish district of Warsaw. There weren't yet any walls separating it from the Polish neighbourhoods and Jewish people could live among the Poles if they could afford it and were able to put up with a certain amount of discrimination. We lived in a three-bedroom apartment that was crowded to capacity even in those normal times before the war, before the Nazis imposed large numbers of occupants per apartment. One of the bedrooms served as the office for the family business during the day and as the bedroom for my cousin Rachela at night. My parents, my sister, my paternal grandmother and me shared the other two bedrooms. The maid, who worked for us from Monday to Friday, slept in the kitchen. During the working day, Mr. Ser, our accountant, spent seven or eight hours in the office. Often, as a reward for something I had been asked to do or for eating food I didn't like, I was allowed to play with the pencils, paper and staplers in the office. I was even allowed to pretend I was calling someone on the telephone. All this was, of course, under the watchful eye of Mr. Ser, who fortunately liked me a lot.

My biggest thrill from this period occurred after my parents took me to a movie starring Shirley Temple. I fell instantly in love with her and asked my father if I could write her a letter on the typewriter; I hadn't yet learned to write by hand. My father agreed and Mr. Ser fed the typewriter with a sheet of our business letterhead. I followed Mr. Ser's instructions as to which keys to press. I typed the letter and "signed" it, and my father put it in an addressed envelope and promised that he would mail it. I'm still waiting for an answer.

The second-biggest attraction in our office, after the typewriter, was the abacus. I was fascinated by the speed with which Mr. Ser used it and transformed his calculations into figures in the ledger. All I saw were wooden rings that he moved like lightning, and I was mystified by the relationship between these movements and the figures he wrote down. When I tried to move the rings myself, Mr. Ser yelled at me and threw me out of the office.

Another adult who was part of my daily life before the war was Rega, one of two daughters in a family of nine children who lived in the apartment below ours. When I was eight or nine, she was in her mid-twenties. Tall, stunningly beautiful with ebony-black hair and a snow-white complexion, she had the curls around her ears that were fashionable then. She wore black (a colour that already appealed to me) because she was in mourning for her late mother. I had a crush on Rega. It took me a little while to figure out when she would come and go, but I then made sure to be on the staircase to say hello. As I write this memoir, Rega is still alive.

The other two people I was close to at this time were the maid, Józefowa, and my grandmother. Józefowa supplied me with all kinds of sweets that I was not allowed to have as payment for helping her with small cleaning and cooking tasks. She also told me endless stories of life in her village, a life that was completely foreign to me.

I could write volumes about my paternal grandmother. She made me feel like the apple of her eye. We communicated in Polish, which she spoke quite well, although Yiddish was her mother tongue and the language of communication between her and my parents. Two things stand out most when I think of her. The first are the many vacations that we spent at her house in Tomaszów, where her garden, full of fruit, was a safe place for me to play. There were dense bushes where I played hide-and-seek with my local Polish and Jewish friends and I rode my tricycle. I spoke only Polish with my friends.

Half of my grandmother's house was occupied by a local doctor who had one of the first X-ray machines in Poland. On special occasions, he would gather both children and adults in his examination room, turn off the lights and ask for a volunteer to put his or her hand behind the glass. The children cried with fear when they saw the bones of the hand through the glass.

The second thing that I remember when I think of my grandmother is the traditional Friday night prayers. Toward evening, my grandmother would put a clean tablecloth on the dining room table and place on top of it a freshly baked challah and two silver candlesticks with new candles in them. Dressed in holiday clothes with a beautifully embroidered handkerchief on her head, she would gather everyone around the table, then light the candles. With her hands over her eyes, she would recite the blessing, making a kind of humming sound and periodically saying a complete word that indicated where she was in saying the prayers. Seventy years later, I can see her face and hear her voice as though it were yesterday. What would follow was a traditional, several-course dinner. A few of my mother or father's close or not-so-close relatives were always invited too. I didn't usually stay at the table until the end of dinner – my mother would bribe me to go to bed by offering me a ride on her shoulders.

I didn't see my mother very often during the week. The family dry cleaning business was in Praga, a suburb of Warsaw on the southeast side of the Vistula River, and my mother most often left our apartment while I was still asleep and returned when I was already in bed. My mother adored me, but it was the entourage of women around me – my grandmother, aunts and nursemaids – who took care of my daily needs and I didn't really develop a relationship with my mother. It was only much later that I realized what a "golden woman" Mummy was: those who knew her remembered her as an example of honesty and diligence.

My memory of my father is that he was the best of all daddies and an exceptional man. He wasn't tall, nor was he terribly handsome – not ugly but no Apollo either. I would say that he was elegant and neat but "neat" is not a strong enough word, and "meticulous" is still insufficient. Daddy was sensitive on the subject of neatness to the point of obsession. It was comical to see him opening and closing the wardrobe three to five times because every time he closed it, he created a draft that would cause one or two of his ties to get caught in the door. He kept opening the door to check that no tie had been caught, which in turn created another draft that would do exactly what he was trying to make sure didn't happen. Sometimes I counted on my fingers the number of times he opened and closed the door before giving up. I ran out of fingers!

That wasn't all. Daddy would brush a hair stubbornly sticking out of his head for five to ten minutes. A hair in his soup was reason enough to boycott the whole dinner. Daddy could find a hole in a perfect sock. If he found one during the week, he put the sock aside and when Mummy came home he would bring her the sock with the darning kit, and, in a very professional way, would pull the sock onto his hand to prove that there was a hole. Mummy, of course, didn't see it and my sister and I would start giggling. Daddy would bring a magnifying glass and call Grandma and the maid for moral support; nobody could stop laughing. In spite of these peculiarities, Daddy was a good father and husband. I never heard my parents quarrel, nor did I ever hear my mother complain about him or about anything else in their life together, even when life became excruciatingly difficult for her.

The age difference between my sister, Niusia, and me was a constant source of conflict between us. I was jealous of her – how could I not be when I heard through closed doors the joyful voices of young people having fun? And no one could wonder at my tears when my sister could stay up and I had to go to bed. Nonetheless, apart from the jealousy, I developed a deep brotherly love for her. It was not reciprocated, though, which is painful for me to remember all these years later. Even now, I think more often of Niusia than of my parents. Perhaps this is because she spoke more often about her will to live.

I have many good memories from my childhood before the war, before the terrible times. One was a visit to Warsaw's beautiful zoo. It was stocked with a wide variety of animals and on such outings Niusia and I were allowed to eat giant portions of ice cream. On one occasion, as I walked along with my parents, I overheard my mother say to my father, "How time flies!" The Polish equivalent is literally translated as "How fast time runs!" I, the little genius, asked my father in all seriousness, "Daddy, does time have feet?" Neither of my parents could stop laughing and admiring my cleverness. My sister, as usual, looked bored. When we passed an artist who would paint portraits on the spot for a small fee, my father said that this event had to be immortalized, which is how I came to have my own portrait above my bed in the bedroom I shared with my sister.

On special occasions, my father liked to show home movies to our family and guests. His filmmaking equipment consisted only of a hand-cranked movie camera, a projector and a screen because, in those days, home movies were silent. Even so, my father was avant-garde; hardly anyone had movie equipment at that time. My family often went to regular movies as well, usually double features, in a hired carriage. I remember the titles of two films that made a strong impression on me. One was *The Hurricane* (1937), a sad story of man against nature, and the second was a science-fiction movie called *In the Year 2036*.

In 1937, when I started elementary school, I met my friend Józek and a deep friendship developed between us from the start. Józek and his family lived a few blocks away from us on the same street, next to a movie theatre. The first time I suggested to Józek that we go to a movie he said that he didn't have the five cents for the ticket and his father wouldn't give it to him for such a purpose. I asked my father if he would pay for Józek's tickets and, in return, I would do additional chores at home. This system worked and we never missed a Saturday matinee showing of cowboy movies with characters such as Tom Mix and the Lone Ranger with his companion, Tonto.

After the movie, we would go to my home, where my grandmother greeted us with cake and milk or soft drinks. After this feast, if my sister was out, we would go to my room and play "cowboys and Indians" for hours. Our horses were dining room chairs that we sat on backwards and our weapons were lassos made from clotheslines, toy tomahawks and cap guns that made a terrible noise and often brought my grandmother to my room to hush us up.

When the Germans occupied Warsaw and began expelling Jews

in 1939, I lost all trace of Józek. To this day, he remains my irreplace-
able best friend.

That, more or less, was my life before the second half of 1939. Our
life passed quietly, without great troubles or great joys. During the
week, everyone was busy working and on Sundays or holidays my
parents often took my sister and me to parks. During the winter, my
father took us sledding. Sometimes on weekends, we would visit our
numerous relatives or just go to the movies. This is the way we were
until the end of August 1939.

The Beginning of the End

As the last acts before World War II began to play out on the world stage in August 1939, the various members of my family were vacationing in different places: my parents were in Romania; I was at a Jewish children's camp in Świder, a village near Warsaw; my sister was at a Jewish camp for teenage girls in Gdynia, a Polish port on the Baltic Sea; and Grandma was at her house in Tomaszów. Three days before the beginning of the war, we were reunited in Warsaw.

On September 1, 1939, regular radio programming was interrupted by the announcement that German infantry was marching into Poland. In a sombre voice, the announcer asked the population to obey the Polish authorities in preparing for air raids. Blackouts, in both the cities and the countryside, were one of the most important elements of this preparation. Blacking out light sources was so important that failure to follow the regulations was punishable by death. Members of the Warsaw civil defence command were given powers to arrest violators. My father and Józiek were among the first to volunteer for this unit.

Aside from scaring us, the first military operations didn't harm us at all. For about three weeks, as the inadequately trained and ill-equipped but valiant Polish military desperately defended Poland, special sirens, broadcast by loudspeakers in the streets, announced the beginning and end of air raids. The inhabitants of Warsaw only went into basement bomb shelters in the last few days of this brave but ill-fated defence, when the Germans began to bomb Warsaw heavily. Most of us stayed in these improvised bomb shelters until Poland capitulated on September 27. Being entirely underground, the shelters offered excellent protection against flying shrapnel, but if a bomb exploded on the building above the shelter there was no chance of survival because the debris buried the occupants alive. On the other hand, many people who did not go down to the shelters soon enough were killed or wounded by flying debris.

As members of the civil guard, my father and Uncle Józiek were also in charge of keeping order, preventing looting and weeding out the *Volksdeutsche* – Polish citizens who were ethnic Germans and spoke both languages. After the war broke out, the *Volksdeutsche* claimed to be more German than Polish and spread fear among the Poles of atrocities that the Germans would inflict on them. Many also openly disregarded the blackout because they wanted the German bomber pilots to see that they were indeed flying over Warsaw.

One of these *Volksdeutsche* lived in our building, in a one-room attic apartment. To our great distress, he played nationalistic German music on his accordion at 6:00 a.m. and refused to stop when asked. My friends and I overheard people in our building discussing the fact that our *Volksdeutsch* neighbour also refused to observe the black-out. It was hard to catch him, however, since every time he heard people approaching his apartment, he quickly turned off his lights. My friends and I decided to watch his apartment from the building directly across from it. Our plan worked and one evening we called my father and Uncle Józiek to arrest him. After confiscating the man's accordion, gun, ammunition, pro-German literature, signs and flags, my father and uncle turned him over to the Polish military police.

I knew that the civil guard had the right to kill any spy caught in an act of espionage and asked my father why he and my uncle hadn't shot our pro-German neighbour. My father dismissed me abruptly, saying something about my understanding this when I grew up.

I saw a dead man soon enough, however. The man had been walking in front of our building looking for a midwife for his wife when he collapsed from his many shrapnel wounds. People carried him down into our bomb shelter and we desperately tried to find a doctor for him. His wounds emitted an awful odour and I could see that he was suffering terribly. His groaning, accompanied by the sounds of gunfire and exploding bombs, the terrible cold and darkness, created an unimaginable scene. We were unable to find medical care and the unfortunate man died the following morning. This was the first time that I was touched by the pain and curse of war.

Along with the horrible, I also witnessed the courageous. During one of the numerous bombardments, a synagogue caught fire and the volunteer fire brigade was able to save very few of the manuscripts and books in the main part of the building. The only civilian volunteer who risked his life to save whatever he could was Mr. Ber, a plain, modest stationery merchant who lived in our building. He continued to rescue the books until part of the ceiling fell down on him, making any further search impossible. His heroic behaviour taught me for the first time what civil courage was and in what kinds of situations it shows itself.

In the first few days of the bombardments, people didn't want to go down to the basement bomb shelters because they were afraid that if the building took a direct hit, they would be buried alive. If they remained in their apartments, they would be exposed to flying glass as well as shrapnel, so they preferred to sit in the stairwells where the risk was reduced by the small number and size of windows. People brought with them anything they thought they would need during the air raids, which could last for a number of hours each day.

Very soon, the stairwells became places where people slept, ate and, for children, played. People dealt with this unusual situation in various ways. There were quarrels about who was taking whose place on the stairs; some people smoked while others screamed at the smokers; some brought pillows, blankets and radios with long cords dragging on the steps. Children were everywhere, chasing tenants' cats and dogs, making lots of noise and having a fine time.

Most people returned to their apartments at night and went about their most necessary business outside during the brief lulls in the bombardments, when a few shopkeepers opened their stores for as long as possible. People would buy their food and check on their relatives because telephone use had been suspended. As the bombardments grew heavier and air raids started at night, the civil guard, under orders from the Polish military command, ordered the civilian population to go down into the basement bomb shelters. People brought clothes, bedclothes, barrels of sand to extinguish fires and any container that could hold lots of water. The air in these closed places became foul from smoking, coughing, body odour and the smell of stale food.

My mother and Rega became self-appointed representatives of the people living in our building complex, who numbered several hundred. They went to food and medicine distribution centres to get as much of these necessities as possible. I was very proud of my mother and father for their civic participation and for the respect and gratitude they were shown by our neighbours.

Toward the end of the third week of the heroic resistance by the Polish army, a ceasefire was declared and the Polish government began negotiations for a conditional surrender. In any event, the surrender became unconditional within a few days. The bombardments stopped, people went back into their apartments and life returned to a certain normalcy. The atmosphere, however, was saturated with the nervous tension of people facing the unknown.

~

I didn't see the Germans marching into Warsaw because I wasn't allowed to go out into the streets, but the next day their motorized units passed right in front of our building. Their arrogance was revealed by the fact that they seemed totally at home. At the head of each infantry unit, a soldier drove a motorcycle with a sidecar containing an officer reading a map and directing the driver, acting as if the whole world belonged to him.

The very sound of the German army's approach sent shivers up and down my spine. When the foot soldiers marched down the streets, the sound of their nail-studded boots striking the cobble-stoned streets of Warsaw was terrifying and could be heard from a great distance.

At first, the Germans' behaviour was very proper as they distributed bread and soup to famished civilians. My family's situation was not among the best but compared to what other people were suffering, we were lucky. Although our office had been slightly damaged by shrapnel from a grenade explosion, our building as a whole was spared heavy damage.

As the German army and the SS established themselves in different parts of the city, rumours began circulating about the SS picking up Poles who were members of the intellectual and professional elite. This included not only military men, but also members of various political parties, university professors, lawyers, doctors and even priests. The procedure was the same in every case. A group of SS men, headed by an officer, would come to the victim's residence with a paper that listed the names of each of his family members, including distant relatives. Explanations were never given for the arrests. No justification was offered, nor was the victim's destination ever stated. Jews of similar status were also arrested, yet at that point we didn't think that Jews were being specifically targeted or that this was the beginning of the same kind of large-scale persecution that had started in Germany in 1935 with the passage of the Nuremberg Laws.

The Germans soon began shedding their masks and signs saying "Nur für Deutschen" (For Germans Only) began appearing in the city. Some streets were completely evacuated and occupied by Germans. Then the raids and roundups began, paralyzing food deliveries, causing price increases and spreading panic throughout

Warsaw. In the beginning, the whole population was targeted and a curfew was imposed on both Poles and Jews. However, the Nazis soon began to target only Jews with taxes, evictions and expropriations. We were inundated with degrading and panic-inducing orders. Two months after the occupation, every Jew over the age of ten had to wear an armband of specified dimensions showing the Star of David on a white background. On the streets, a Jew had to step down from the sidewalk, take off his hat and bow to an approaching German.

The Jews of Warsaw were consumed with anxiety about what the future might hold. There were two schools of thought about how to respond to the situation: those who believed that they should remain in Poland and those who believed that the only way to survive the war would be to flee to the Soviet Union. In 1939, before invading Poland, Germany had signed a non-aggression pact with the Soviet Union and the two powers had divided Poland between them. As the German invasion pushed eastward, the Soviets moved westward and occupied their pre-arranged part of eastern Poland. This created an opportunity for many to take advantage of the chaos and flee to the Soviet zone.

The question of whether to stay or flee also affected my parents. They had heated discussions about it in Yiddish so my sister and I wouldn't understand what they were saying. My father had relatives in Bialystok, on the Soviet side, and since we couldn't reach them by phone or mail, my parents decided that my mother would go in person and get more information about life in the Soviet Union. A day or two after she left for Bialystok, however, my sister and I were awakened by my father, who told us that he had to join my mother without saying why. I began to cry and begged him to take us along. My sister turned to face the wall and went back to sleep. My grandmother started praying and weeping. Rachela put her arm around me, but I was inconsolable.

In the end, my mother came back and my father was the one who remained in Bialystok. He was unable to return to Warsaw until after Germany invaded the Soviet Union in June 1941.

During my parents' absence, Rachela ran the shops, Grandma managed the household and my sister and I flitted around like two butterflies. My sister was at the vulnerable age of fifteen and since the schools were closed, we had no supervision; we were doing things our parents would not have allowed if they had been home. My sister began running around with young men and women, a group known as the "golden youth" who took advantage of the social disorder to hold unsupervised get-togethers.

I was no better. Although I was only nine going on ten, I began smoking cigarettes, pestering girls, fighting in the streets and, in short, behaving badly. Together with other boys and girls my age, I tried to imitate the "golden youth." We searched for the basement lockers belonging to people who had disappeared or been captured by the Germans and raided them, looking primarily for radios. In one of their first publicly posted orders, the Germans had demanded that all radios be turned in to them. Anyone caught with a radio would be shot on the spot. We sold the few radios we found on the black market and with the proceeds bought cigarettes, stylish clothes and other items for our amusement.

When we had exhausted the supply of radios, we graduated to selling *objets d'art* and silverware; sometimes we filled special orders from "clients" – adults who lived in the Jewish district. Very soon we had non-Jewish customers who were mainly skilled workers employed by the city. One of their tasks was to remove all the iron, copper and other metals attached to walls and buildings in Warsaw so it could be melted down and used for the German war machine. While they were working inside the Jewish area, there was constant commerce between us. Some adults followed our lead and engaged in similar trade. Among the popular items sought by Jewish customers were foods unavailable in local stores.

Our most popular item, though, sought by everyone, were sleds. During the winter season, which in Warsaw lasts from four to six months, everyone used sleds to transport almost everything. We built them by stealing attic floor boards, removing the short planks that joined the supporting beams, sawing them to the right length and width and manufacturing runners from the metal bindings on barrels. This was my first real business venture.

My mother's return home partially interrupted my new way of life. I began attending a school that had been started in the Jewish district and having private lessons, and life resumed some sort of normalcy. But we missed our father, who was forced to remain in Bialystok.

Persecution

During the summer of 1940, not long after my mother returned to Warsaw, the Nazis began establishing a walled ghetto and by October, ordered all Jews in Warsaw to move into the area. We didn't have to move because our apartment on Dzielna Street was within the designated ghetto boundaries. Our plant in Praga had been confiscated and changed into a factory manufacturing Christmas ornaments. I don't know if it was confiscated by Germans or by Poles with connections to the German authorities, but confiscation was one of the aces that the Germans held in Poland, as they did elsewhere. It was easy for the Germans to divide and conquer – the Jewish population and the Polish majority had had little positive contact and most did not trust each other.

We also had to close two of our three stores. The first was closed because it was outside the ghetto boundaries and, although the ghetto was not yet sealed, we weren't allowed to live or work beyond its borders. The second store, located on Gęsia Street, was confiscated by the newly formed Jewish council and given to another entrepreneur. Our third and main store, on the same street as our apartment, was diagonally across from Pawiak prison. We often heard bursts of gunshots that lasted for over an hour coming from there. Every time these "concerts" finished, the infamous black trucks known as black Berthas – to the horror of everyone in the ghetto – would leave the prison full of dead bodies.

Even worse, when the black Berthas were empty, the drivers en-
tertained themselves by roaring onto the ghetto sidewalks at high
speed, killing or injuring anyone who got in their way. Soldiers stood
on the running boards holding "lollipops" – the signs used for directing traffic – and hit people in their path, then drove away laughing,
leaving the destruction behind.

Amidst this chaos, my still-energetic mother set up a makeshift
dry cleaning plant in our apartment. She put a gigantic wooden tub
to wash the clothes in benzene in the middle of the dining room and
hung the garments to dry on cords installed from wall to wall. The
clothes were then ironed by a hired helper, a father of six children
who had been expelled from his small village near Warsaw. As time
went on, though, the price of benzene, now only available on the
black market, rose astronomically and our already reduced business
eventually became impossible to carry on.

Despite becoming increasingly grey and thin, I never heard my
mother complain. She was always available to help anyone who asked.
Her father, who was now very old, and two of her brothers often came
to our house for meals. Looking at them made it clear that starvation
was at hand for everyone in the ghetto. Although this could not have
been later than 1941, our relatively fortunate family had already sunk
deeply into hardship.

By this time, gossip was already spreading that the Nazis were
about to begin dealing drastically with the Jews. The air was filled
with a strange atmosphere – the way it feels before a storm. We felt
the sword of Damocles hanging over us and had no idea when it
would fall. Day after day, more and more frightening posters were
plastered on the ghetto walls containing an ever-increasing number of edicts and degrading, life-sized caricatures of Jews with huge,
crooked noses and claws in place of fingers.

By early 1941, great numbers of Jews from the areas around
Warsaw – and even from Lodz – were being forced into the Warsaw
ghetto with only the possessions they could carry. A new German

directive ordered the ghetto population to share their apartments with this influx and the housing situation became a burning problem. Every room had to be occupied by a different family and huge numbers of these refugees were forced to live on the street. Life in the ghetto was extremely difficult. Around this time, my mother's brother Kuba, his wife, Aneczka, and their son Stach were expelled from Lodz and came to live with us. We also had to share our apartment with another family of four, which made a total of eleven people living in a three-bedroom apartment where my mother was trying to run the family business.

On June 22, 1941, Germany attacked the Soviet Union in a Blitzkrieg campaign. Despite a number of very reliable warnings, Stalin had not prepared his army for a German attack and the highly motorized, mobile, well-equipped German army was able to advance several hundred kilometres eastward almost without opposition. The German offensive on the eastern front, according to their propaganda machine, was fast, brutal and very successful. Their victories were touted in posters on every wall and in every official Polish and German newspaper. On almost every poster, a caricature of a Jewish face was shown on a mythical animal with claws drinking the blood of a poor Christian victim.

The positive aspect of these events for us was that since Bialystok was now under German rule, my father could return to Warsaw, even though it took almost all our remaining valuables to bribe officials and obtain the necessary papers to bring him back safely.

Happy as we were to have my father with us, his return added one more to the number living in our apartment and, with our presser coming every day, it was impossible for my parents and Rachela to earn enough in our dining-room dry cleaning plant for us all to survive. Luckily, we had been able to move all our customers' clothes into our one remaining store and could sell or barter whatever was unclaimed. The selling was usually between us and other ghetto residents; the bartering took place between us and the Poles working in the ghetto.

People like our family who, despite our crowded situation, were still in our pre-war lodgings were the object of jealousy. The overall conditions in the ghetto are hard to imagine and the situation worsened with the continual arrival of increasingly huge numbers of newcomers; contagious diseases spread and lice, tuberculosis and starvation contributed to a large number of deaths every day. I contracted typhoid fever – then called stomach typhus – but was miraculously saved by my grandmother. I don't know what remedy she used.

The people who had been forced into the ghetto from nearby villages and small towns lived on the street, in attics or in basements. Often they had used up whatever money they had from selling or bartering their belongings and could no longer buy food. Their situation was tragic. These people, along with thousands of others, were starving to death, dying in the streets. At the beginning of this terrible period, passersby would stop near the dead person and cover him or her with newspaper. As these deaths became an everyday occurrence, people stopped paying attention and left the bodies lying uncovered in the streets; it was often several days before the Jewish crews came to bury them in common graves in nearby fields.

Dozens and dozens of small, naked children stood or sat or lay against the walls too hungry even to speak, their eyes silently begging for something to eat. I remember their swollen bellies and their bodies covered with scratches from the lice that attacked them.

One of the ways in which starving people made a desperate effort to survive had elements of a hunter stalking his prey. A person would stand near the door of a shop that sold food, pretending to be part of the passing crowd. The minute a customer left the shop with his purchase, however, the desperado would jump on this person, grab the food and run away. When the people who were still able to buy food started holding on to it more tightly, the *chappers* (snatchers) would bite the food they were carrying. This took place most often with bread since it was bought without wrapping. Of course, after the food had been bitten, the purchaser simply surrendered it to the *chapper.* This kind of encounter often attracted small crowds, members of which were divided between those supporting the buyers and those supporting the *chappers.* Very often, these incidents ended in melees.

Aside from starvation, many suicides and other premature deaths occurred because of the inhumane conditions. Yet, in the ghetto, in mid-1941, you could still buy anything and everything to eat or drink if you had the money. You could even secretly attend concerts given by classical musicians. And on the few occasions when I walked in the ghetto with my father, young women would grab my father's arm and rub it against their bodies, softly asking him to follow them. Some of my friends who were older than I explained the meaning of these encounters and I began to be able to identify the prostitutes by the clothes they wore and the way they held their purses. At the age of eleven, I became an expert at spotting them and started to associate this activity with a certain pleasant excitement.

To further demoralize us, the Nazis formed "anti-lice" units composed of non-Jewish Polish women who were escorted into the ghetto by the Jewish police. In full public view, they systematically went from building to building and ordered all the occupants of each apartment to come down into the courtyards for an inspection. The inspections always ended with these female barbers cutting off the hair of those assembled whether lice was found or not. Some men were relieved to get rid of their lice, but nearly all the women put up a terrible, physical fight against this public humiliation inflicted on them.

Since November 1940, the ghetto had been enclosed by high walls topped with pieces of broken glass and barbed wire. There were only seven or eight gates, which were guarded by armed German soldiers and by Polish and Jewish policemen, and you had to have special written permission from the German authorities to enter or leave the ghetto. These restrictions, however oppressive, created an opportunity for smugglers, who were both individuals and organized gangs.

A new industry was born – food and everything necessary to prepare it were smuggled in, and objects of value such as clothes, gold, silverware and *objets d'art* were smuggled out.

This trade in goods could be very lucrative, but it was trumped by the money that could be made by smuggling people. Some Jews could afford to bribe authority figures to get false identity papers, although the process was complicated and extremely risky. The interested party would have to be introduced to a *macher*, an influential person, who could obtain the false ID of someone who was dead or had never existed. Next, the *macher* would have to get a requisition from the German administration for the labour or services of the Jewish person in question. After the almost impossible job of getting these papers, which could take months, the person had to present him or herself, with the papers, to the German officer at the gate. The *macher* used his knowledge of the German officers and their duty hours at the gate to choose the time and day when an officer who was less likely to check the authenticity of the papers was on duty. No matter how hard everyone concerned tried, there were frequent arrests and killings at the gates. Still, none of this deterred desperate people from trying to get out.

Life on the Polish side exposed people to dangers from the human hyenas who preyed on them. Jewish men were caught more often than women because being circumcised made them easier to identify. Blackmailers extorted whatever they could from their desperate victims and, as soon as the Jews' money and valuables had been exhausted, they turned them over to the Gestapo, often for the price of a small bottle of vodka.

It was clear by now that the Germans had won the political war against the Jews. At the beginning they had recognized our rights, gaining our confidence. Then they had gradually taken away our rights and imposed ever-increasing hardships. Some people thought that they were carrying out new, stricter orders from Berlin. Others believed that they were executing a pre-determined plan that was now revealed in its brutal totality for the first time. Whichever it was, life went on and some people even managed to profit from this terrible situation. The few who still had money and connections with powerful people in the ghetto administration also controlled the price of food, other necessities and, most importantly, access to false papers for those who were willing to take the enormous risk of trying to escape and survive on the Polish side of the walls.

The atmosphere in the ghetto streets was rapidly degenerating. Afraid of being rounded up for forced labour or worse, people avoided going out even for necessary errands. Apartment buildings in the ghetto were connected to each other through attics or basements, so people broke through these connecting walls to go from building to building, and even from street to street, without being seen from the outside. When the new phase of German and Jewish police brutality began, the more enterprising inhabitants set up counters and tables in basements and attics to sell and barter, and life went on again.

During a period of relative calm, my sister met Peryk (Peter) Dawidowicz, a Polish-speaking German Jew who had been expelled from Germany just before the war and had settled in Warsaw. It was love at first sight for my sister and I hero-worshipped Peter from the start. I saw him almost every day and, because of our relative closeness in age, I found I could identify with him. I was especially impressed by the way he dressed, with leather jackets, coats, boots and, most unusual among Jews, a Tyrolean feathered hat.

About this same time, I lost my dearest *confidant*, Józek. It happened without warning – one day when I went to see him, strangers answered the door and told me that his whole family had disappeared. I have never found another friend to replace Józek, which was why I sought and received special attention from Peter. Using pencil and paper along with his hands, feet and voice, he showed me how to start an engine by cranking it up from the front and how to work the clutch, gas and brake pedals. For the next few days, after learning the necessary functions by heart, I sat on a chair (since we had no car) and drove everyone crazy with the noise and gestures of my "driving." This allowed me to forget my favourite game of playing cowboys and Indians with Józek.

Peter also taught me, very tactfully I realize now, the "facts of life." One day, as we were both urinating, I asked him the question that burned in the minds of most boys my age. Since I no longer believed in the stork, I asked him how babies were made. After a few seconds of silence, Peter gently explained the truth of the matter, even though I couldn't understand everything then. He promised me that when I reached seventeen or eighteen, Mother Nature would help me understand, as she does for everyone. This answer satisfied me for the moment, but I began to look at couples differently and conversations with my few remaining friends concentrated on this new topic, spiked with all kinds of possible (and impossible) sexual scenarios.

What made me idolize Peter even more was a hair-raising exploit of his. On a dare, he rode a bicycle through an open, but guarded, gate out of the ghetto. The watch on this gate consisted of armed German soldiers and Polish policemen as well as Jewish policemen who were sometimes armed with rubber clubs. Peter risked being shot and killed, or at best wounded. He got through the gate but as he was tearing away on his bike, he was hit by a bullet on the ring finger of his left hand. He managed to elude the guards and seek first aid through his Polish friends who were waiting for him in a Polish neighbourhood outside the ghetto. After this, I saw Peter as a hero and told this story to everyone. As I look back, I realize that it also changed my attitude toward escaping our enemies. I began to see it as possible.

Struggle for Survival

When the Jewish ghetto administration, called the Judenrat, or Jewish Council, and the Jewish police force were formed, everyone assumed that the Council was set up to serve as a liaison to the Germans, and that the main function of the Jewish police was to keep order in the ghetto. The Germans, however, had other plans for both organizations.

In July 1942, the Germans informed us of our impending "resettlement" in the east. Under the pretext of keeping the streets free of the homeless in order to prevent the spread of disease, they solicited volunteers for "resettlement," offering them bread and jam as a gesture of "good faith." I now believe that the near-starvation conditions in the ghetto had led my friend Józek's family to volunteer for "resettlement" – the Nazis lured people not only with bread and jam but with promises of employment. They also announced that the Jewish police would be responsible for organizing the efficient evacuation of these volunteers.

Accordingly, the Jewish police organized transportation from the centre of the ghetto to the train terminus, which had already become known as the *Umschlagplatz* – the collection point. We saw long, open, horse-drawn carts filled with early volunteers holding their bread and jam and small bundles of belongings, each cart guarded by two or three Jewish policemen. Some of the young volunteers sang, as if to prove to themselves and onlookers that taking up the German offer would improve or even save their lives and that they were happily embarking on an outing.

It's important to understand that many men joined the Jewish police to earn a living and, because the force performed a useful function for the Germans by serving as a buffer between the ghetto and the "Aryan" part of Warsaw, many survived longer than would otherwise have been the case. And while it was not uncommon to see a Jewish policeman dragging one of his own relatives to the *Umschlagplatz*, assuring the victim that he or she would survive the war in a labour camp, we also witnessed acts of heroism and devotion. Some of the Jewish policemen who were forced to take their own families to the *Umschlagplatz* removed their caps and belts and jumped onto the carts to share the fate of their loved ones.

By this point in 1942, although we didn't know it at the time, whole Jewish populations of towns and villages had been sent on trucks and trains directly to the death camps in various parts of Poland. Many thousands of Jews had already been murdered in their villages and towns and buried in mass graves, the locations of which were only officially revealed after the war. Killing squads – called *Einsatzgruppen* – had been dispatched to villages where they rounded up the Jewish population and forced them to march to the edge of an open pit and undress before being shot into the pit. Then they forced Jews they had spared or Polish peasants from nearby villages to cover over the graves. Not all the Jews were dead before they were buried.

After the many volunteers for "resettlement" left, the ghetto remained extremely crowded because their places were immediately taken by new arrivals from nearby small towns and villages. When the number of volunteers for "resettlement" had dwindled to a point unacceptable to the German authorities, the posters on the walls no longer asked for volunteers but instead ordered designated groups of Jews to report to the *Umschlagplatz*, supposedly for transport to labour camps. Now the penalty for disobedience was death. We were in a panic. We couldn't understand this sudden shift in policy from voluntary resettlement to forced deportation since, of course, we had no idea about the early 1942 decision of the Nazi leadership to implement the "final solution to the Jewish question." Now both the Jewish police and SS officers were responsible for filling quotas of people to deliver to the *Umschlagplatz*. The scenes in the streets became uglier as Jews were dragged from the streets, stores and apartments and herded into the horse-drawn carts. Despite the cries, screams and fights, in the end, the daily quotas were met.

Just as we thought that things couldn't get worse, people learned that the highest official in the Jewish ghetto administration, Adam Czerniaków, killed himself in response to a diabolical order to deliver six thousand Jews, including children, to the *Umschlagplatz*. Fear and insecurity permeated the ghetto and paralyzed its inhabitants.

The Germans responded to Czerniaków's death by ordering the Jewish police to round up people indiscriminately. For reasons unknown to me, some people, including my father, found out the date of this raid. For the first time, I began to panic. We had been receiving a steady stream of information from Polish train engineers who operated trains that went to Treblinka and from the rare Jewish escapees. These two groups of informants had no contact with each other, yet their stories about what was happening to Jews corresponded exactly. We now had no reason to doubt that once in the *Umschlagplatz*, we were doomed. The possibility of being sent there and then shoved into overcrowded, standing-room-only cattle cars kept me in a state of hysteria all day.

My father suddenly changed from being undecided and irresolute to being energetic and resourceful. As the leader of our family and the small group of people who depended on us, he gathered us together and announced that we would all move to our store on the corner of Dzielna and Karmelicka streets and hide in the basement. It had no toilet or stove, but did have running water. In preparation for the move, my father ordered us to gather as much ready-to-eat food as possible; we would enter our hiding place at night through the rear door that was invisible from the street and stay there until the raid was over. My mother and grandmother wanted to wait inside our apartment for a few more days, but my father refused and preparations began at once.

We sent a message to my father's brother Arthur, his wife, Marysia, and their son, Tolek, informing them of our plan and urging them to join us. We warned them that unless they came immediately, they would not be admitted – the store would be locked and the jalousies (the louvred shutters) drawn to give the impression that the store was empty.

My uncle and his wife arrived a few hours before the time when my father had promised to lock the door. To our surprise, Tolek didn't come with them. When my father took his brother aside to ask why, my uncle got angry and told my father to mind his own business. He nervously lit a cigarette and went into a corner of the basement, where we heard Aunt Marysia crying and fighting with him. After my mother intervened, Marysia calmed down and explained that Tolek had refused to follow them, saying that the raid was a false alarm and that people would be perfectly safe in their own apartments. He argued that the only people who would be caught and deported were the homeless poor. A heated argument between father and son had resulted in Uncle Arthur slapping Tolek. According to Marysia, Tolek was very hurt, and to get revenge against his father, he had dashed out into the street.

After the raid, witnesses told my uncle and aunt that Tolek had voluntarily jumped onto one of the collecting wagons. To this day, I don't know what happened to him. Aunt Marysia had a nervous breakdown and lost her voice, and her marriage with Uncle Arthur ended. We lost all contact with her and had no idea of her fate. This event marked the first time the extended Ney family fell victim to the Holocaust.

When we returned to our apartment after the raid, neighbours told us that Peter Dawidowicz had been standing in front of our apartment when the Jewish police stopped in front of the building with a wagon half-filled with victims. One of the policemen demanded to see Peter's identification papers, which had always been considered "strong," giving him license to move around the ghetto more freely than anyone else. Peter had tried to explain that, since it was a hot summer day, he had left his jacket and papers in his fifth-floor apartment.

Peter's father, a doctor in Germany, had saved the life of the father of the man who was now a high-ranking German officer and commandant at the Pawiak prison, which gave him a certain amount of confidence in dealing with the Germans. Peter had kept in touch with the commandant and we had met him months before when, on Peter's recommendation, he came into our store and asked my mother to clean his leather gloves. When the commandant came back for his gloves a few days later, he chatted with my father in German. My father translated for the rest of us and his words still fill my mind with horror. Very calmly, as though discussing a movie, the commandant impressed upon my father that everyone deported from the cities, towns and villages of Poland would be made into soap. He added, however, that since he had a moral debt to Peter's father, and thus to Peter, he would be willing to ensure the survival not only of Peter, but of my sister as well. At that moment, my sister moved closer to Peter and put her head on his shoulder. My father, scanning our faces, had politely but firmly refused the offer.

After speaking to the people who witnessed Peter's capture, my father hired a bicycle-drawn rickshaw and ordered the driver to take him to Pawiak prison. We tried desperately to stop him, to no avail. When we saw the rickshaw entering the main gate of the prison, my mother broke down in tears. Niusia was visibly upset and I had tears in my eyes. A crowd gathered around us and speculation was rife. To our great surprise, the rickshaw soon emerged and sitting beside my father was the commandant. As they passed us, my father yelled that they were going to the *Umschlagplatz* to find Peter and bring him back to the ghetto. When my father returned a few hours later, however, the look on his face told us that we would never see Peter again.

~

After the raid in the summer of 1942, people on the street looked worried and tired; almost everyone had somebody who had been taken to the *Umschlagplatz* and never heard from again. The raids and deportations continued for weeks and the number of people left in the ghetto dwindled dramatically.

In August, the Germans issued a notification that the ghetto area would be reduced: Nowolipie, Nowolipki and Leszno streets would be relegated to workers and most of the other streets had to be emptied, the windows and doors boarded up. Anyone found in the condemned zones after the deadline would be shot on the spot. Jews were permitted to remain on several other streets because of the brush factory there that the Germans wanted to keep open. This area became known as the "small ghetto" and the people who lived and worked there became known as the "brushmakers." The empty streets that surrounded and separated the "big" and "small" ghettos became known as the "wild" ghetto.

Two of the streets that were spared were controlled by German industrialists. Nowolipie Street housed the Schultz Firma owned by Fritz Emil Schultz. As a war production company, the Schultz plant cleaned and repaired German army uniforms sent back from the eastern front infested with lice and with pieces of human flesh stuck to the cloth. During the winter months, as Soviet planes flew overhead, thousands of German soldiers lay face down in the snow in their white uniforms to avoid detection. The Soviet pilots had orders to save ammunition by flying slowly in circles long enough to cause the German soldiers' elbows and knees to freeze solid and, in many cases, for them to die of exposure. When the uniforms were taken off the wounded or dead soldiers by the German medics, the frozen skin tore off their bodies and stuck like glue to their uniforms.

Leszno Street belonged to Walter Caspar Többens, who manufactured textiles as well as leather goods, mainly coats and boots. One of the pre-war buildings on Leszno Street was the City Court, architecturally a great source of pride. Built on several square blocks, it faced the ghetto on one side and, on the other side, faced "Aryan" Warsaw. No matter how hard the Germans tried to seal the building, smugglers managed to use it as a conduit between the ghetto and the outside.

During this terrible time, my father again showed his capacity as a leader. He refused to accept the German order that everyone who lived in the condemned streets report to the *Umschlagplatz* and wasted no time in looking for someone to help us survive. Anyone who worked for Schultz or Többens had the right to remain living on one of the streets on which the factories were situated. We would have to obtain a requisition for our labour and then find a place to live on one of the legal streets. By this time, our household consisted of eight people, a fact that, even if we could get the labour requisition, made the search for an apartment a seemingly impossible task.

Then a miracle happened. By talking to the right people and telling them about their experience in running a dry cleaning plant, my parents obtained the necessary requisition for three people – my father, my mother and my seventeen-year-old sister – to work for the Germans. I was too young to be a legal worker and my grandmother was too old. Uncle Kuba and his wife were too sick and Rachela did not have the Ney family name. My father also managed to get a requisition for a fourth-floor apartment on Nowolipie Street that consisted of one room and a windowless alcove. It was again my father's decision that we stay together and take our chances that the war would be over before the Germans discovered there were eight of us living there. Gathering whatever we could carry, we left our apartment on Dzielna Street forever.

As the streets emptied out, the chaos was indescribable. People streamed toward the *Umschlagplatz* carrying what they considered to be their most essential belongings. Others packed their suitcases in an orderly fashion and marched there like soldiers. People came from all directions and some, disoriented, even walked in circles. There were cries, shouts and fights, sparked by any and every disagreement. Thousands of people were walking to the trains and thus to their death. It was a living hell.

Life in the new ghetto fell into a pattern under draconian rules. There was a twenty-two hour curfew: people were legally allowed to be on the streets for only one hour in the morning and one hour at night, to walk to and from their places of employment. Anyone on the street outside these hours would be shot. It didn't take long before we found ways of moving around in attics and basements similar to the system we had used in the larger ghetto. People used these passages as central places to communicate, putting up notices, for example, asking the whereabouts of their loved ones. Once again, the passages were used to carry on a brisk trade that would supplement the starvation rations provided by the Germans. The work the Jews did for them was entirely slave labour, without wages of any kind.

The Nazi authorities cut off all electricity to our living quarters, forcing us to invent other means of heating, lighting and cooking. For lighting, we made a kind of acetylene lamp by putting small pieces of a gas-producing carbon into a metal can and then dripping water onto the "stones." The flow of water was controlled by a screw at the top of the can and as the water touched the pieces of carbon, the gas escaped through a small hole in the top. When we lit the gas with a match, it produced a bright flame along with a hissing sound. We could control the brightness by increasing or decreasing the amount of dripping water. It was a wonderful invention that made our lives literally a little brighter.

For cooking, people used any wood that they could find: we tore wood from the outside of buildings, from the floors of attics and basements, and from the shelves and doors of unoccupied apartments. Later, when the cold weather approached, we constructed stoves made from open metal barrels with small metal pipes pushed through a hole in the middle of the base. The barrels were filled with sawdust packed tightly around the pipe so that when the barrel was closed and the pipe removed, the sawdust could be lit through the hole in the bottom of the barrel. The small amount of air coming in from the bottom kept the sawdust smouldering from the top down. These devices produced wonderful heat for a whole room and some people even managed to connect pipes that would heat more than one room. We also used them to keep food warm.

Squeezing eight people into one room, a kitchen and an alcove was unbearable. My father, who was so fastidious that he would normally never wear any piece of clothing two days in a row, was now obliged to wear the same clothes for weeks at a time. It was impossible for anyone to be clean by pre-war standards and eventually everyone was infested with lice. My father was constantly running his hands inside his shirt, picking up and squeezing the lice between his thumbnail and any hard object, killing them. I don't remember seeing other vermin in our crowded quarters. Most likely, there was never enough food on the floor to tempt cockroaches, much less mice or rats.

The alcove in our new apartment had a small opening facing an empty lot that stretched about one hundred metres from our building and ended in a cul-de-sac. I think that the lot had contained a lumber mill before the war. No one standing in this empty lot and looking at our building would suspect that there was a room behind the tiny window. My grandmother decided to put our alcove and the similar spaces on the three floors below ours to use. She bricked up the entrance to the alcove in each apartment, then painted each wall the same colour as the rest of the apartment, making it impossible for anyone to know that there was anything behind the walls.

Along with the tenants of the other apartments, my grandmother then decided that there should only be one door through which the tenants could enter the alcove sections of the building. A square was cut out of the attic floor above the top alcove and the wood was made into a cover with a small handle that fit perfectly over the hole. We camouflaged the whole thing with glue and feathers from the many pillows left in the attic. It didn't look suspicious because the rest of the attic floor was covered with feathers, blankets, drapes, towels, fabrics, pieces of clothing and suitcases that had all belonged to the people who had come and gone, never to return.

Now that the shelter was built, my ambitious grandmother needed to make it a place where people could hide for a few days at a time. Food and water had to be brought in, bunk beds installed and a minimum of clothes and household implements provided. The three tenants living below us were very skeptical about my grandmother's proposal and offered no help, saying that they had to spend their time trying to find food and other necessities for themselves. However, they did not forbid my grandmother from working in their apartments since she had all day to do it, being "illegal" and therefore non-existent in the eyes of the Germans. When the alcove walls were completed and painted, the three tenants openly wept, thanked her and apologized for not helping.

Everyone sat around the table in our apartment and compiled a list of necessities to bring into the shelter. There could be as many as fifty hiding there, counting the tenants from all four floors plus others nearby who might force their way in. For the next few weeks, people brought so many items into the shelter that my father had to padlock the trap door.

～

In our overcrowded apartment, Uncle Kuba and Aunt Aneczka slept on a small cot in the kitchen, and the rest of us slept on two double beds. My uncle became a prisoner to vodka, but not in an unpleasant way – he became a raconteur of interesting and funny stories. My aunt, however, developed tuberculosis and kept everyone awake at night with her constant cough. Their son, Stach, visited them every day and brought what little food he could get from his mysterious sources to be shared among all of us.

Stach was always energetic, enterprising and full of hope, which contributed greatly to our morale. My parents asked him many times where he slept and one day he finally told us. He had met a well-known physician, Dr. Płocker, who lived with his wife at 25 Leszno Street, and had formed an immediate friendship with both the doctor and his wife. Dr. Płocker had become Stach's mentor and the secret as to where my cousin slept at night was revealed. This put an end to the rumour that he had a mistress, though he may well have had one since he was charming, intelligent, knowledgeable on a wide range of subjects and resourceful.

Stach was determined to get his parents to the "Aryan" side of Warsaw and save their lives. Using his wide-ranging connections, Dr. Płocker had secured a promise from a few non-Jewish Polish families to take care of Stach's parents. They would have to be hidden separately, but that was the best that could be done. Although Stach arranged for excellent false papers with his parents' pictures, one problem remained: by this time his mother was bedridden and was completely unable to walk through the ghetto gate on her own. This is where Stach's resourcefulness came into play. He knew of a man who was in charge of a group of Jewish labourers working for the Germans outside the ghetto. They were all strong young men who left the ghetto every morning and re-entered it at night.

According to Stach's plan, his mother would be put into the middle of the column as it approached the gate. After the man in charge had presented papers for all the workers, my aunt would be lifted up between two men and simply carried through to the other side. The plan included diversions to prevent the Germans from noticing and bribes to the Polish and Jewish police to make them look the other way. It worked! Uncle Kuba was also able to join the marchers, having stayed off vodka for a few days before the escape.

Even before this daring escape, Stach had contributed to our family's survival in other ways. In late 1942, we were starving – the three official workers in our group were trying to feed the eight people living in our tiny apartment on their starvation rations. Stach discovered that there was a cellar full of potatoes under one of the buildings in our courtyard. The ghetto administration was supposed to distribute the potatoes, but Stach had found out that they were instead being sold on the black market at exorbitant prices.

One night, after attaching a long, sharp knife to one end of a long broom handle, he laughingly announced that it was time for Turek and him to test his "spear." The potato cellar had two or three small, barred windows without any glass, but even a small child like me could not fit through them. We waited until midnight before silently sliding down the staircase banisters to the courtyard in our stocking feet and then moved along the walls to the opposite side of the courtyard. Stopping in front of the first little window, we used the spear to pull out potatoes and within a quarter of an hour had three full bags. We couldn't slide back upstairs to the apartment, so we crept along the walls of the staircase to minimize the squeaking. I don't remember how long it took, but it seemed like forever. In the excitement I suddenly had to answer the call of nature and, of course, had a slight accident.

The next day, Stach put a small number of potatoes inside his shirt and went out to barter for whatever other necessities he could find. Unfortunately, our source of potatoes only lasted a few days. The people Stach bartered with noticed that all the potatoes had identical cuts in them and when we went back a few days later to repeat our harvest, we found to our dismay a long queue in front of each window. Within a few days, the ghetto administration boarded up the windows, forcing us to say goodbye to potato soup.

One day, we all woke up to find a notice plastered on all the walls ordering everyone, under pain of death, to report for a selection. The Germans claimed to have received information that "illegal" (i.e., non-working) people were living in this rump of a ghetto. The posters assured that people with work permits would not be punished and would be able to remain in Warsaw. Strangely enough, the few days that the Germans gave us to report to the address in question gave my family time to decide what to do. We knew that regardless of whether we reported as ordered or hid, our family would eventually be decimated. My grandmother's shelter might hide us for a few days, but we were sure that the Germans would in time discover us and force the three "legal" members of our family to witness the deportation of the rest of us.

Just as we were debating what to do, Stach appeared and told us that he had a plan. There was apparently a hiding place in Dr. Płocker's apartment that was large enough for all nine of us to stay in for a few days. There was a wall made of expensive wood panelling and hung with coat hooks along a wide hall that ran the full length of the apartment and no way to see that a panel slid open into a long narrow space furnished with benches and chairs. If the Germans intended to keep the ghetto open for work as before with people who returned from the selection, it was safe to assume that hiding for two or three days would serve our purpose.

After much discussion, we decided to hide in Dr. Płocker's apartment because it was located in a building on the side of Leszno Street that had been officially empty for months; very few people would see us going in the direction opposite from the selection. There would also be less chance of anyone following us than would have been the case with our own shelter. Stach took command and instead of walking as a group of nine, we went one by one to the doctor's apartment. We didn't carry any luggage so it would look as if we were going to the selection. At this point, people had been told not to take any belongings to the collection point. After a few hours we were all in place and Stach, who was the last to arrive, slid the wooden panel closed behind him. The one small attic window in the hidden room provided air and a view onto the roofs of the lower buildings around – a Protestant church and a small section of Leszno Street with the ghetto wall. No one could see us, even if we stood at the window. Gradually, the street became quiet and for the first few hours, our plan seemed to be working.

Suddenly we heard noise coming from Leszno Street. Cautiously peering down toward its source, my father saw a large group of drunken soldiers stagger to the door of the church and use their rifle butts to break it down. After a few minutes, they emerged carrying rolls of fabric and odds and ends that no one would expect to find in a church. Stach said the church must have been used as a warehouse and abandoned when the ghetto walls were built around it. The soldiers began to sing "Heil Hitler! Warschau judenrein!" (Warsaw is free of Jews!) and unsteadily walked away, leaving the fabric behind.

There were only a few leftovers in Dr. Płocker's kitchen and once again, Stach saved the day. He realized that if the people who left for the selection were not allowed to take anything with them, any food they had must still be in their apartments. The surest way to find food would be to go from apartment to apartment and take whatever we could. Instead of giving us hope, though, thinking about this made us more depressed. After hearing the drunken singing of the soldiers who looted the church, we thought that this was really the end of the Jews of Warsaw. And we knew that our isolated little group could certainly not survive alone.

Suddenly, my father, who had been watching from the little window, whispered excitedly that there were people walking down the street in small groups. They didn't look as if they were coming from a selection – there were some children and old people among them. We decided to go down and find out who these people were, where they were coming from and where they were going. They told us that they all worked for Schultz or Többens and that the people in charge of the selection had sent them back. The few old and very young people had come out of hiding to join them.

We decided that our best chance to get food was still to go from apartment to apartment. Since Nowolipie and Nowolipki streets were still "legal" because they were occupied by workers, Stach concluded that we should look among the apartments that were now outside the shrunken ghetto. These apartments would be empty, since their inhabitants had either been forced to leave or had volunteered to do so.

At first, my father refused to give me permission to go, but Stach and I eventually prevailed and set out on our hunt. As we walked along Leszno Street, Stach looked through the windows of various buildings with an appraising eye. When I asked him why, he answered that he was evaluating the quality of the furnishings because we would have a better chance of finding food in the apartments of the wealthy.

Entering the courtyard of a clean, undamaged building, we started climbing the exterior staircase. The first door on the first floor was unlocked and we found ourselves inside an apartment that looked more like a general warehouse than a single-family dwelling. Every room was packed with dry goods, clothes, paintings, silverware and an enormous quantity of flour, canned goods, jam, sugar, salt and oil. Stach said that the occupant must have been a highly placed official in charge of distributing food to the workers, who had used his position to hoard these supplies.

Stach and I went to work. We emptied two suitcases from among the many that were in the apartment and loaded them with the food that we thought would be relatively easy to carry and to prepare. It didn't take long since we were limited to the two suitcases. As we dragged the suitcases toward the open gate that led to the street, however, we were stopped by a group of people coming into the courtyard. Many of them were crying and wailing. One of the women looked at us and our luggage and screamed, "Thieves!" The group stopped and a few men with fierce expressions on their faces came toward us. There were cries of "Hang them!"

Stach told the crowd to open the suitcases to see what we had taken. He said that if they found anything but bare necessities in them, they could indeed kill us. He also told them to look at the apartment that the food had come from and see for themselves the kind of people from whom we had "stolen." It would be clear to anyone, he said, that the supplies there had been illegally hoarded. He added that they themselves had probably been the victims of these hoarders. Some of the people in the crowd were sympathetic and persuaded the others to spare our lives. They said that our stealing was a tragedy, not a crime, and that by killing us they would be acting just like the Germans. We tried to leave with the two suitcases, but the group only allowed us to take one. Nevertheless, the food was a life-saver for our starving relatives.

Shortly after this incident, Stach escaped from the ghetto with his parents in the courageous manoeuvre that I have already described. Although Stach continued to visit us for a while, we lost contact with him and I don't have any idea what happened to him or his parents.

Brushes with Death

In early fall 1942, my father went to work early one morning without waiting for my mother and sister, saying that he was behind in his work. The rest of us were still in bed when we heard a voice, speaking through a megaphone first in Polish and then Yiddish, ordering us in the name of the German authorities to come down to the street and await further instructions. We were given three minutes to present ourselves. My mother told my grandmother to hide in bed, and rolled her in the heavy duvet against the wall. My sister didn't wait for my mother and me – even though the weather was mild, she grabbed her lightweight coat and ran out of the apartment.

When my mother had finished camouflaging my grandmother, she told me to grab a bottle of water and a piece of bread from the table, then pushed me toward the door. On the second floor, we were met by soldiers with machine guns who yelled, "Schnell, verfluchte Juden!" (Hurry up, damn Jews!) A minute or two later we were standing in the street with hundreds of people waiting for the next order. We weren't allowed to stand on the sidewalk, where soldiers in various uniforms stood guard. This indicated that several ethnic groups were being used for this operation; even within the SS, soldiers from different countries wore uniforms of different colours.

Every so often, one of the soldiers beat someone for no reason – in some cases these beatings ended with the soldiers shooting and

killing their victim. Soon we were ordered to start marching. A row
of German soldiers with dogs ran along each side of the column to
make sure that we kept moving. We still had no idea where we were
going. My mother held onto my hand, the one in which I was holding
the bottle of water, and I had put the piece of bread inside my shirt. To
my surprise, the column turned onto Dzielna Street, passing in front
of our original apartment building. In my distraction, I dropped the
bottle of water and fell down, creating a bottleneck. People around
me were yelling, stumbling and falling.

I felt my mother pull me up and drag me behind her. The Germans
were now making us run rather than walk to catch up with the rest of
the column. As I was running, holding onto my mother, I felt something touch my right temple. When I looked up, I saw the point of a
gun against my head and behind the gun the face of a very young soldier. My mother pulled me toward her and then pushed me forward.
This apparently satisfied the soldier, who dashed off to some other
part of the column.

Until this point, I had not seen any Jewish police, but when we
entered the *Umschlagplatz*, we saw Jewish policemen armed with
wooden truncheons. They ordered us to form new columns, four
people abreast. On each side of the first four people stood a Jewish
policeman who placed his club across the chest of the two people
closest to him, preventing them from moving.

My mother and I were in the third or fourth row. A few hundred
metres from us stood a freight train normally used to transport merchandise or animals. This time, however, it was packed with people.
Every so often, a German soldier near the train gave a hand signal
and the two Jewish policemen at the head of the column moved their
clubs and pushed the next four helpless victims into the train. In a
few moments, my mother and I were next in line.

If the reader believes in miracles, what happened next was a
miracle. The German soldier responsible for filling the train turned
around to face us and lifted both hands to indicate that there was no

more room. The two Jewish policemen told the rest of us to go back into the *Umschlagplatz* and disperse. People started walking around aimlessly, trying to make some sense of the situation. Why were legal workers for German-owned factories being deported without being allowed to take anything with them? It was at this point that people began to realize that not work but gas chambers awaited us all.

Up to then, I had not felt any specific fear. After hearing what was being said around me, however, I was sure that the hundreds of people who had not yet been shoved into a train would be sent on the next train that could arrive at any moment. I did not want to die in a gas chamber. I would have to find a place to hide.

There were several buildings surrounding the *Umschlagplatz,* including warehouses and the back entrance of a hospital. My mother and I were walking around the square, scanning the crowd for my sister. Suddenly, I spotted Niusia and another young woman not far from us, surrounded by people who were calling to them, saying, "Sister, sister!" When Niusia had grabbed her coat as she was leaving our apartment, I remember thinking that it was silly because the temperature didn't require one, but that coat ended up saving her life. In the *Umschlagplatz*, she had put the coat over her shoulders like a cape, with the shiny blue lining facing out, which made her look like a nurse. In Poland, as elsewhere, nurses were called "sisters." I cannot describe how relieved we were to see Niusia alive and not in any immediate danger.

The woman with Niusia really was a nurse who could go in and out of the hospital. She had managed to get the identity papers of a nurse who had died a short while before and gave them to Niusia, who could use them to return to the ghetto at the end of the nursing shift. After some tearful goodbyes, my sister left us, promising to find my father. We didn't know what had happened to him at the Schultz factory. Niusia said she would also do everything possible to help us get back to the ghetto – our apartment there now seemed our most likely safe haven.

My mother and I continued moving through the crowd, not sure what to do until Niusia returned. I was looking around for a potential hiding place when I spotted two small children, a boy and a girl, no older than seven or eight. The girl was holding her little brother's hand protectively as they marched straight toward me. When they reached me, the girl said, "Pani Ney [Mr. Ney, a very respectful form of address], a piece of bread, please!" The piece of bread she was asking for was in my hand, but I refused and walked away. More than sixty years later, I fight the guilt that still weighs on me. I've realized that I didn't refuse to give the children my bread because I was hungry but because I was terrified that I might find myself starving later if I survived all alone.

I rejoined my mother, who was standing in front of the open doors of a warehouse. The floor inside was covered with feathers, clothing, dead animals and excrement, along with wall-to-wall furniture, tools, piles of wood and drawers. The stench was abominable, but I went inside because I thought that we could find somewhere to hide. The huge amount of feathers came from the pillows that Jews used to hide small objects of value that they thought they would be able to carry with them. In reality, the Germans forced people carrying pillows to open them and empty out the contents. I left the door to the warehouse open so that no one else would be tempted to enter and wade through the mess.

Inside the warehouse, I spotted an enormous grandfather clock standing in a corner. The space inside the clock was large enough for my mother and me to sit, so I persuaded my mother to get into the clock with me to hide until the Germans had finished loading the next train. A few hours later, toward evening, a new train arrived. We heard the cries and screams as the train was packed with its human cargo and then left in the direction of one of the death camps. The *Umschlagplatz* fell silent. As my mother and I emerged from the clock, we saw one of the hospital's back doors open and a man appeared carrying a pail. After he had thrown its contents onto the ground and lit a cigarette, we approached him and my mother told him our story. He said that there already were a number of people hiding in the hospital and he could not guarantee our safety, but he was willing to let us spend the night sleeping on the hospital floor.

The next morning, we left the hospital, trying to blend in with the others who had been hiding there and walked over to a group of Jewish policemen. My mother took off her wedding ring, asking loudly if any of the gentlemen would accept the ring as payment for delivering a message to my father. One of them accepted, so my mother gave him the address of our apartment, mentioning as well that he might be at the Schultz factory. She added she was willing to generously pay anyone who helped her return to the ghetto.

As I listened to my mother talk to the policeman, I understood that my situation was totally impossible. There was no way that a small boy would be allowed to go from the *Umschlagplatz* to the ghetto; I was completely illegal. I was beginning to despair when another miracle occurred. A young woman appeared from nowhere and approached us with outstretched hands. "What are you doing here, Mrs. Holcman?" she asked. My mother told her about the morning raid and our seemingly hopeless plight. The woman listened carefully and then, in a tone that left no room for argument, said that she could save me but not my mother. I looked at my mother in desperation. I wanted to believe the woman but did not want to abandon my mother. The woman was in a hurry. My mother kissed me tearfully and off I went holding the woman's hand, not knowing where we were going or how she planned to save me.

At the exit from the *Umschlagplatz* the woman was stopped by Jewish and Polish policemen, who asked for her identification. In an official-sounding tone, she told one of the men to fetch the German commandant of the *Umschlagplatz*. About fifteen minutes later, the commandant arrived and kissed the woman on the cheek. In a tearful voice, she told him in German that her whole family had been taken away on the trains and that I, her nephew, was the only survivor. She begged him to let me go with her to her apartment in the ghetto. Turning to the policemen, the officer ordered them to raise the barrier and I walked to freedom.

It turned out that the woman lived next to our building. She took me straight to our apartment, where we found my sister, my father and, to my great surprise and happiness, my grandmother. Using his connections among the Jewish police, my father managed to negotiate a ransom for my mother. The mystery lady, who had indeed lost her whole family, turned out to be the mistress of the German commandant.

~

Life in the now-decimated ghetto went back to as much normalcy as was possible under the circumstances. People worked longer hours to make up for the loss of their workmates; both the Schultz and Többens plants were very busy around the clock. Niusia was slowly getting over the loss of Peter Dawidowicz, but did not try to replace him. As for me, I was free all day to go more or less wherever I could without being seen by either Germans or the Jewish police.

Coming back from their shift one evening, my parents met Uncle Arthur on the street accompanied by a woman they had never seen before. To the delight of my grandmother, my parents invited them to our apartment, where he introduced the woman as his new wife, most likely for the benefit of my sister and me since it was unclear how they could have gotten married. Uncle Arthur told us that after he and Aunt Marysia had left our store, devastated by the loss of Tolek, Aunt Marysia had died of a broken heart. He and his new partner were living in the "small" ghetto.

There was no question of serving them dinner since there wasn't enough food for anyone and since we couldn't invite them to stay overnight in our apartment, the time came to say goodbye. My uncle's lady friend asked my parents to let me go with them for a few days so I could eat better food and get more sleep because conditions in the small ghetto were better. The prospect of eating and sleeping as much as I wanted overcame my anxiety at being separated from my family and although my grandmother cried, my parents agreed. We left my family's apartment soon after and walked for about an hour through a maze of attics and basements of empty apartment buildings to our destination.

I remember hearing arguments between my father and his brother before the war in which my father called my uncle a liar. I never learned what my father was accusing Uncle Arthur of lying about, but this time my uncle certainly kept his promise – I was indeed well-fed, washed and had my own bed with clean sheets. Although the apartment had only one room, for a few days I lived in a relative paradise.

While I was staying with Uncle Arthur, we heard a loud speech coming from the courtyard and joined other tenants to listen to the man in charge of the makeshift bakery on the ground floor of the building. According to information from his connections among the Germans who ran the brush factory, another raid was coming. I was frightened and started to cry, asking my uncle to take me home because the Germans were expected at any moment. To my surprise, instead of running away, the tenants from the building calmly entered the bakery, as did my uncle and his companion, who held my hand tightly.

Once everyone was inside, the man in charge walked over to the wall that contained the oven, around which were shelves and other articles necessary to bake bread. When he pushed a loose board on one side of the oven, the oven began to swing on an invisible axis, revealing a large room with more than a dozen benches. We all went into the room and the man, whose name I never learned, returned the oven to its original position, leaving us behind it. Only the leader remained outside – I learned later that he was a liaison between the German authorities and the Jewish population. He had been ordered to deliver anyone in his building who was illegal to the *Umschlagplatz*, but because some of his family would have fallen victim to this order, he took a chance and allowed everyone to hide in the secret room behind the oven.

Inside the room, a young man told us that he was a member of a recently formed underground unit. Our hiding place was very safe, he said, but we must remain in total darkness and complete silence – we couldn't sneeze, cough or smoke. If the Germans discovered us, he added, he would go down fighting. To emphasize his point, he pulled a German Luger from a hidden pocket. There were about twenty-five of us in the hidden room, including a young mother alone with an infant.

We didn't have long to wait until we heard voices and the hammering of German military boots. "Soweit, und kein Jude mehr?" (So far, then, no more Jews?) The question was directed at our saviour who answered in German that all the Jews in the brushmakers' ghetto had already been taken away. I was sitting next to the young man from the resistance and became aware of perspiration running down his body onto my arms. When I accidentally touched his arm, I realized that he had the gun in his hand. Then we heard a dog begin to bark and, to our horror, the baby wake up. Then silence. After a few seconds, we heard the German soldiers leave along with the man in charge.

I had once more narrowly escaped death. After about half an hour, the bakery man returned, opened the hidden room and told us we could go home. People ran out, laughing and crying and kissing each other, especially our hero, who had shown nerves of steel. Suddenly, the crowd became quiet. The last person to emerge from the bakery, moving slowly without looking at anyone or anything, was the young mother. She was holding the corpse of her infant. She had smothered it to save everyone else.

Not long after that incident, my uncle took me home. It didn't take long for me to get used to my previous life again but I soon got bored with not being able to go outside. Things were a little better at night when my parents came home from work and people would gather in the attics to discuss politics, our chances of survival, the latest crimes, and predictions as to when the war would end. Even skeptics now agreed that the Soviet army was closer to Warsaw than they had been a few months before. Some people even made predictions as to when the Soviets would enter Warsaw, basing their estimates on German newspaper reports of "strategic withdrawals and regroupings." There were whispers about a Jewish military unit in the ghetto who would take up arms, who were willing to die rather than be slaughtered. The discussions also included a certain amount of spicy gossip about some people's infidelities, but there was very little, if any, physical violence among our group. The attic gatherings provided space for people to barter for food, the most important commodity, as well as personal hygiene articles, false papers, clothing, cigarettes and vodka.

Smuggling was a necessary part of ghetto life. I already knew that, although I didn't realize how many of the traders were young boys and girls of my age or a bit older. They were easily distinguishable from the other kids their age. With full stomachs and round cheeks, they didn't look hungry. The clothes they wore were simple but clean and they made an effort to look like Polish kids. The boys sported long hair that they constantly tossed back with a sharp sideways movement of their heads, a gesture typical among Polish boys. Most of the girls had hair bleached with peroxide that constantly needed touching up and they wore tight-fitting clothes, shoes with high heels and as much makeup as possible. The biggest problem for both boys and girls was speaking Polish without a Jewish accent – it was virtually impossible because almost everyone spoke Yiddish at home.

I listened as these young smugglers told stories about fooling the German soldiers at the ghetto gate, selling articles to non-Jewish Polish clients on the "Aryan" side and buying a variety of items at minimal prices. The boys, of course, had another topic that dominated all others – their sexual exploits. It was as though I were in a huge classroom with many teachers presenting subjects that I didn't understand. I decided that I wanted to find out more about this group and if possible join them. I started spending most of my time at the place where the smugglers congregated in the morning and at night, the only times when people were allowed to be on the street. One of the boys eventually noticed me and, being a little older, assumed the role of my mentor and protector. He took pleasure in telling me how well he had done on this or that day and explained the principles of smuggling.

One day, my mentor (whose name I unfortunately do not remember) proposed that I go with him to bring back cigarettes to sell in the ghetto so I could see if I liked smuggling and was good at it. If it worked out, he promised he would teach me everything he knew, introduce me to his connections outside the ghetto and show me where we could spend the night. If we waited to re-enter the ghetto in the morning, he explained, we could do business both with workers going out to their jobs and on their way home at night.

I was very interested in taking him up on his offer but said that I couldn't understand how the smugglers were getting in and out of the ghetto. My mentor laughed and answered that if I didn't want to bribe my way through the gate, I could crawl through one of the many holes in the wall surrounding the ghetto. He warned me, however, that I might face dangers other than the Germans and the police on the "Aryan" side – Polish hoodlums, usually drunk, often waited outside the walls to rob or kill young Jewish smugglers or turn them over to the Germans. Every smuggler had to have his own Polish "protector," someone who, for a small fee, would make sure that we could conduct business without being harassed. There were a few instances of bloody fights between one hoodlum protector and another. The winner then became the new protector of the other smuggler.

I was eager to try my hand at smuggling even though it was clearly a game where the odds were against the smugglers. In the last few days of my mentor's preliminary instructions, there were several fatal shootings of young smugglers by Germans. Nonetheless, it was time to make a decision. Although I didn't consider myself all that brave and had always avoided fights with other boys, I had been presented with an opportunity to help my starving family. The fact that my newfound friends were smuggling successfully was also something of a challenge for me and I wanted their approval.

The next morning, I gave my parents an excuse for leaving early and told my mentor that I was ready to start. The workers were on their way to their jobs, so I would have to take their orders, go to the "Aryan" side, fill the orders and come back to the ghetto in time to conclude the transactions as the workers returned. I was very nervous and when I'm nervous, I stutter, which amused my comrades. My mentor took me aside, offered me a cigarette – which I refused – and explained how we would get out of the ghetto. He also gave me fifty złotys so that I could bring something back. We crossed Nowolipie Street and headed for the Leszno Street gate, where we encountered a Jewish policeman, a Polish policeman and a heavily armed German soldier.

My mentor explained that he would approach the Jewish policeman and tell him that two people would be going through. After a short bargaining session, a price would be set that included bribes for the Polish policeman and the German soldier. We would have to wait for the Jewish policeman's signal – according to my mentor, the Jewish and Polish policemen would always accept a bribe but this was not the case with German soldiers. The promised signal would usually be given when a huge truck or a horse-drawn wagon passed through the gate so that we could go through on the side opposite from the German soldier. That way, if he was being watched by the SS or the German military police, he could claim not to have seen us.

That first morning, there were a few smugglers waiting ahead of us for an opportunity to approach the Jewish policeman and we had to wait about half an hour for our turn to speak to him. The minute the Jewish policeman gave us the sign, we would have to walk, not run, through the gate. That was exactly what happened. We got our signal when a huge horse-driven wagon loaded with a pile of boxes passed through the gate going into the ghetto. As soon as we got to the other side, we were surrounded by Polish people coming and going in every direction. I felt exhilarated but shaky.

The meeting with our Polish contacts was two blocks from the gate. Seeing that I was a little scared, my mentor put his hand on my shoulder and assured me that the second time would be a piece of cake (if I lived that long). As soon as we reached the meeting place, he immediately started trading with the Polish buyers and sellers. I also noticed the Pole who was to be our protector. When our business was finished, I said that I wanted to buy a box of cigarettes for my father, which made everyone laugh since cigarettes were available in the ghetto.

We had to stay outside the ghetto until the workers returned in the early evening, so that we could use the one hour that the curfew was suspended to sell what we had bought and take new orders. My mentor also told me that he would introduce me to Mr. Serafinowicz, a Polish man who allowed smugglers to stay overnight in his apartment across from the small ghetto, for a fee. He had to give a few złotys for each smuggler to the janitor of his building, who promised, in return, not to betray the smugglers to the Germans. The janitor, unfortunately, was a drunk, and could be unreliable. Nonetheless, this arrangement allowed smugglers to double their profit – in the morning we could take orders in the ghetto, sell items from the ghetto to Polish people outside and buy items to fill our orders; the following morning we could sell the items we had bought to the crowd going to work in the ghetto. On this first day, however, I insisted that we go home the same day because I knew that my family would be frantic. I must admit that I was also excited about telling them of my exploits.

The Serafinowicz apartment was one large room with two double beds, a few chairs and an old table, plus a bathroom and an alcove for the stove. Mr. Serafinowicz looked about thirty years old, as did his wife, and their three children ranged in age from about five to nine years old. Later on, there were five smugglers who used this apartment periodically – four boys, including myself, and one girl. Whenever any of us stayed overnight, the family slept in one bed and we used the other. I took an instant liking to Mr. Serafinowicz and sensed that the feeling was mutual.

The few hours that we spent outside the ghetto went by very quickly. We discussed politics and, as usually happened when Poles wanted to show their good will toward us, we heard that they had a distant ancestor who was Jewish. Finally, the time for our visit was up and we shook hands. Mrs. Serafinowicz asked me if I could possibly bring some of the discarded clothes that were strewn all over the streets of the ghetto for her children the next time I came.

On our way out of the apartment, we passed the drunken janitor, who took off his hat with one hand, bowed and stretched out his other hand for the "rent." When we arrived back at the gate, the traffic in and out of the ghetto was heavy enough for us to sneak inside by walking on the far side of a truck, unseen by the German guard. A few minutes later, I took the steps to our apartment two at a time and walked in to see my family sitting in complete silence. After a few seconds, everyone started to scream and fire questions at me. My father took me by my shoulders and tearfully called me every name imaginable as he had never done before. Then he sternly told me to sit down and explain where I had been all day. Without a word, I pulled the package of cigarettes that I had bought for him from under my shirt and placed it in front of him. The brand was almost impossible to find in the ghetto and was very expensive. My father gave me a strange look – a mixture of puzzlement, affection and admiration. When I had finished my story, there was silence and then, as if by an unseen command, my whole family got up from their chairs and began to hug and kiss me, laughing and crying. At that moment, I grew by at least a metre.

My father disappeared into the kitchen and came back holding two glasses and half a bottle of vodka. "Although you're not a man yet," he said, "you have almost behaved like one, so here is your chance to complete your initiation." He filled both glasses with vodka and handed me one of them. Lightly clinking my glass, he exclaimed, "L'chaim!" (To life!) and emptied his glass in one gulp. I repeated my father's words but hesitated a second before swallowing the vodka. I knew I had to do it, so I did, in one gulp like my father. I don't remember anything after that because, as my mother later told me, I immediately fell unconscious onto the nearest bed.

Our life continued amid the sombre and worried mood in the ghetto. We had the constant feeling that something was coming. Some people still believed that the Germans wouldn't destroy the unpaid labour they needed to replace their own workers, who were fighting on one of many German war fronts. Another group, however, were beginning to realize that Hitler considered the annihilation of the Jews to be a mission that had to be completed at all costs.

As the days went by, I became more and more experienced at smuggling and, as a result, braver. I cultivated my own clients, new and more direct sources of merchandise and, what I considered most important, connections with reliable Jewish policemen. I also joined a group of smugglers who were protected by someone I considered to be the most powerful, honest and likeable protector.

Out of necessity, we had to buy from Polish suppliers who were near the ghetto gate. We always had to be on guard and, with each transaction, bargain for every złoty anew. In the ghetto, however, our best buys came from the ordinary people who were desperate to survive. One of the hottest items, besides gold, jewellery and small *objets d'art*, was the ordinary wringer attachment for a washtub. Every abandoned Jewish apartment had had at least one and as smugglers sold them to the Poles, their price doubled because they were one of the items most in demand outside the ghetto. They were very heavy and cumbersome to carry, but many times, when I knew that the German soldier on duty at the gate liked me, I ran through the gate carrying two wringers. In my short career as a smuggler, I built a monopoly in buying and selling wringers for washtubs.

There were also sad days when young smugglers were caught and beaten by Polish hoodlums for not wanting to pay the usual bribes. These were boys and girls who took a chance and refused to join the groups who had Polish protectors. One day, my protector failed to show up outside the gate and I was caught, beaten and hit on the head with sharp objects. If one civilian Pole had not taken pity on me and fought off my attacker, I would most likely have been killed.

Exit

In April 1943, a beautiful Polish spring was beginning to make itself felt. People appeared in the street wearing lighter and fewer clothes. Our smuggling industry was receiving orders in preparation for the approaching religious holidays of both Passover and Easter. One day, my father gave me an unusual order: he wanted me to bring him a certain German newspaper that specialized in reporting battles on the different fronts. I was surprised that he wanted it because this newspaper was so widely known to be full of propaganda that even the German soldiers openly made fun of it among themselves as well as with Poles and Jews. When I asked why he didn't want a Polish underground newspaper that was always available on the street, my father laughed and replied, "You have to read between the lines." Sure that I had caught my father in a mistake, I answered with some superiority, "There is nothing but white space between the lines!" The next day, however, I brought my father two newspapers, one German and one Polish underground sheet and he explained that analyzing the lies of the journalists in the German newspaper and catching the "facts" that were known from other sources to be false enabled him to get a pretty accurate idea of the actual situation on the eastern front. For example, the "strategic withdrawal" to a new position only a few kilometres away from a former position was in reality a huge retreat, sometimes as much as twenty kilometres in one day. In addition,

since there were no reports of advancement on the eastern front, you
didn't have to be a genius to realize that the front would very soon be
in Poland and with it, liberation.

As Passover approached, my grandmother miraculously transformed our one-room apartment into a festive place. In recent weeks
I had spent most nights at the Serafinowicz apartment in order to
buy and sell twice a day, but I promised my family that I would spend
the Passover holiday at home. On the day before Passover, April 18,
1943, my parents and sister went to work as usual and we said goodbye to each other with "See you soon!" Since it was too early for me
to go through the gate, I spent the time talking to my grandmother
and asked her half jokingly what she would like me to bring her for
Passover. Very seriously, she replied, "Garlic."

When I arrived at the gate an hour or so later, I witnessed something that I had never seen before. Because of the time of day and
the approach of the two holidays, no people or goods were passing
through the gate in either direction. The two policemen and the
German officer were standing together, looking relaxed and deeply
involved in conversation. The German soldier's machine gun, which
was normally held at the ready, was hanging on his back and when he
noticed a few smugglers standing near the gate, he just waved them
through. After a little hesitation, we ran through the gate.

Since I had already decided that I wouldn't go back to the ghetto
until the following morning, I went to the open market to buy the
promised garlic. It didn't take me long to find a peasant woman selling produce and I spotted a string of garlic. When she asked me how
much I wanted, I was nonplussed. My grandmother hadn't told me
how much garlic she wanted, so I said, "The whole string." The market woman looked surprised and something about her faint smile
made me realize that she somehow knew I was Jewish. After I had
paid for the garlic, I told Mr. and Mrs. Serafinowicz the story because
I was worried that I had put myself in danger. They burst out laughing
and explained that Poles didn't use much garlic so they only bought

one or two cloves at a time. It was widely known, however, that Jewish cooking called for a lot of garlic, so a boy buying a whole string of it must be Jewish. The Serafinowiczes congratulated me for sensing the danger and suggested that in future, when I found myself in new situations, I avoid speaking to people I didn't know.

When night fell, the Serafinowicz family lay down on one bed and another smuggler and I lay down on the other. Sometime near morning, Mr. Serafinowicz shook me awake saying, "Get up! Get up! The ghetto is burning!" At first I didn't think that it was any big deal since there were often fires in the ghetto, but he insisted that this time was different. Despite the curfew, he said, crowds of people were in the streets and shots were being fired from the ghetto. That did it. I jumped out of bed, got dressed and pulled the cover off my bedfellow, yelling, "The Jews are shooting at the Germans! Get up so we can find out what's happening!" Outside, we were among hundreds of people in the street. We saw individuals framed in the windows of some of the ghetto buildings shooting at German soldiers on the "Aryan" side. The soldiers were taking cover in a merry-go-round that had been brought to the square in preparation for the Easter holiday, hiding behind the wooden horses.

My fellow smuggler and I exchanged looks in silence. One of the ghetto buildings closest to the wall had been hit by incendiary shells and was on fire. It was burning from the bottom up and since no one was putting out the fire, it was only a matter of time before the building collapsed. Suddenly, someone in the crowd started yelling, "A woman! A woman! She's going to jump!" I turned my head in the direction that everyone was looking and witnessed the image that later became one of the "official" photographs of the Warsaw Ghetto Uprising, probably taken by a German photographer. I saw the woman standing on the roof of the burning building wrapped in a flag; after shouting something I couldn't make out, with flames already at her feet, she jumped to her death. The crowd gasped in unison.

My comrade and I followed Mr. Serafinowicz home as the Polish police dispersed the crowd. It was already morning and no one went back to sleep. We sat at the table waiting for someone to start talking. When we finally broke the silence we all agreed that this was an extremely dangerous situation, that it was impossible to predict what would happen next.

My comrade (whose name I'm afraid I don't remember) seemed to be less worried than I. He had told me that he had entrusted everything he had to a Polish maid working for a German family and assured me repeatedly that she had promised to give him back all his money any time he asked for it. I remembered that when I had earlier told my father my friend's story, he had warned me that such "caretakers" were almost never reliable.

As I write this memoir sixty-seven years later, I can still remember how desperate I felt, how tragic and hopeless my situation seemed to be. Here I was, a twelve-year-old boy who was suddenly separated from his whole family, relatives and friends. I had no place to stay and knew no one among the Poles except the Serafinowicz family. I had very little money and no idea where to go and what to do. It was a beautiful spring day, but looking at the burning ghetto and hearing the gunfire from both sides prevented me from feeling even a moment of happiness. I almost burst into tears, but my will to live got the upper hand and I began planning my next move.

My comrade left the apartment, saying that he might not be back for the coming night. I felt the need of Mr. Serafinowicz's advice. I told him that, unlike my friend, I didn't know anyone on the "Aryan" side to whom I could turn for help, although I did have the birth certificate of a Polish boy of my age, Piotr Grodzieński, who had apparently died in Treblinka. When I started my smuggling operations my father had bought the document for me from a woman who worked for the Grodzieński family, saying that one day it might save my life.

Mr. Serafinowicz assured me that I could stay in his apartment for a few days and I thanked him for his generosity, realizing that I was putting his family's lives in danger. I also told him that I needed

to find out if there had been shooting in my parents' neighbourhood – in the Schultz and Többens ghetto separated from the "small"
ghetto by empty streets – which would mean that Jews in both ghettos were participating in an organized uprising. Mr. Serafinowicz,
however, said it was much too dangerous for me to go anywhere near
the larger ghetto where the chances of my being recognized as a Jew
and a smuggler were enormous. At the same time, remaining in his
apartment with the drunken janitor close at hand was risky for all
concerned. He suggested that I instead go to a suburb of Warsaw and
stay with one of his relatives.

The idea of getting away from Warsaw appealed to me immediately and I agreed to stay with his relative for a few days until we could
re-assess the situation in Warsaw. A few hours later, a young woman
opened the door of a single-level apartment house and welcomed me
without objection. I later found out that this woman already knew
about Mr. Serafinowicz's relationship with smugglers and was not
surprised to hear my story. When her father came home that evening,
he told me that I could only stay for two days because the toilet was in
an outhouse and no matter how careful I was, a neighbour might spot
me and turn us all in to the Germans. I was so concerned about it that
in the two days I was there, I only went to the outhouse once, in the
middle of the night, to minimize the danger of discovery.

A few hours after my host left for work the next morning, his
daughter said that a visitor would be coming around midday and I
should hide in the kitchen broom closet. I could see through cracks
in the closet door and soon saw a postman come into the apartment,
take off his jacket and hat, and sit down at the table while the young
woman served him tea with bread with jam. For some reason, this
made me think of stories that other smugglers had told me about
men and women, and a strange excitement ran through my body. I
glued my eyes to the cracks and soon enough saw what I had heard
about: for the first time in my life, I saw people having sexual inter-
course. To my relief, the love-making soon ended and the couple sat

at the table talking and drinking tea. The postman picked up his bag, kissed the young woman on the cheek and left. A few minutes later, she opened the closet door and told me that the coast was clear.

Her father came home early that afternoon and said that it was too dangerous for me to stay any longer. He was worried that sooner or later a neighbour would spot me, even in the middle of the night. I wasn't surprised to hear this since I hadn't felt secure from the moment I arrived. Strangely enough, I had felt more secure at Mr. Serafinowicz's apartment in Warsaw, even though it was objectively a more dangerous situation. I was always conscious of paying attention to the people I met, not just the situation, in order to detect danger.

It wasn't long before I was back at Mr. Serafinowicz's table telling him about my brief adventure. I felt trapped, as I had felt on many other occasions in the ghetto, overwhelmed by the paralyzing fear of the unknown. This time, Mr. Serafinowicz decided that a farm would be the best destination for me, since farmers always needed help at this time of year. He knew that I had spent many summers as a child either at my grandmother's house in the country or at a Jewish summer camp near Otwock, a town about twenty-four kilometres southeast of Warsaw that was surrounded by farms.

Like a drowning person grasping at straws, I began to feel more hopeful as I imagined my life on a farm. To take advantage of the lengthening spring days, we decided that I should leave for Otwock immediately. Mr. Serafinowicz gave me directions and I set off. I arrived in Otwock in early afternoon and knew right away that I couldn't stay there – there may have been farms around it, but they weren't immediately visible.

I wandered through the town, trying to be as inconspicuous as possible, until I eventually found myself near a deserted beach with water on one side and bushes on the other. Mrs. Serafinowicz had given me a piece of chicken wrapped in paper, but I wasn't hungry and decided to hide it to eat later. The fact that the beach was a bit out of the town, and that I could hide in the bushes, made me think I could spend the night there. I found a place to bury the chicken and started looking for a better shelter. After a disappointing search, cool night was approaching and I realized that I couldn't sleep outside. I returned to where I thought I had buried the chicken and realized angrily that I couldn't find it.

I was now both hungry and cold, and knew I would have to ask for shelter at one of the few houses near the beach. I began to walk and, to my horror, I found myself in the middle of a cemetery; for the first time since my escape from the ghetto, I began to cry. The path through the cemetery led to a group of houses and, gathering all my courage, I knocked on the first door. As Mrs. Serafinowicz had solemnly told me I must do, I gave the man who answered the obligatory Christian greeting, "May Jesus Christ be glorified," waited for him to answer, "For all eternity," and then said, "Amen," in unison with him. I told the man the story that I had learned by heart: my parents had been killed in eastern Poland by Soviets (a fact that no one could check) and I could no longer stay with a distant relative of my father. I explained that I was looking for employment on a farm for the season.

The man was visibly upset. He told me that he had neither work nor a place for me to stay, but went inside and came back with a piece of bread. I ate the bread as soon as the door was closed. It was my first taste of the homemade type of bread that I was soon to know well. Resuming my search for a place to stay, I decided that I should try to find a more secluded house away from the road. I walked on in the gathering dusk and soon found myself in front of a large house with an even larger extension in the back.

I repeated my story to the man who opened the door and, to my surprise, he told me that I could sleep in his barn. I followed him to the dark structure in the back, where he told me to sleep on a pile of hay and to cover myself with an old coat lying nearby. Wishing me good night, he left the barn, closed the door and, to my great alarm, padlocked the outside. All kinds of scary thoughts raced through my mind: I saw the man returning in the morning with German soldiers to kill me. I went through different scenarios, but they all ended the same way. Had I had experience on farms, I would have known that the padlock was not to keep me in, but to keep thieves out.

The barn was almost completely dark, but, luckily for me, it was a clear night with a full moon that shone through the cracks in the walls. Walking along the walls and touching them with my hands in the semi-darkness, I looked for an opening that I could squeeze through. Eventually, I found a broken board that I pushed outward to make an opening large enough for my body. Feeling satisfied, I lay down near the hole, covered myself with the old coat and tried to fall asleep. Sleep didn't come, but instead I endured a second wave of dark thoughts. I worried about how fast I could disappear through the hole when the farmer brought the Germans to kill me.

The local trains would start running between Otwock and Warsaw in the early morning. I decided that I couldn't work in Otwock because there weren't really any working farms there – my host and his neighbours lived on big pieces of land where they grew vegetables and kept a few small animals for their own consumption. They didn't need hired help to do this. I knew that I had no choice but to return once more to Mr. Serafinowicz's apartment in Warsaw. If I wanted to leave before the Germans or police arrived, it would have to be at the break of dawn. The only problem was that I didn't have a watch. I could only hope that my uncomfortable sleeping accommodations would wake me up early. These were my last thoughts before I fell into a deep sleep.

I woke up as the sun was slowly climbing over the horizon into a slightly foggy, then blue sky. I wasn't sure whether it was late enough to go to the train station and I didn't want to hang around a deserted train station during the Easter holiday – that would surely arouse suspicion and provoke unwanted questions. Suddenly, I heard a rooster crow and, soon after, as if they had been waiting for the signal, other roosters joined the choir. They were joined by the other farm animals, all calling for their breakfast. "This is it!" I said to myself, brushing the dust and hay off my clothes. I squeezed out of the hole and soon was walking through the empty streets of the town. At the train station, I looked at the clock near the list of schedules for the holiday week and was upset to see that I had a few hours to wait until the first train to Warsaw. I found a bench outside that was off in a corner far from the main entrance and almost cut off from public view. Although I was still cold and hungry, I covered my eyes and started to doze.

I was awakened by a strange sound that was neither speech nor singing coming from a drunken man who was holding an almost empty bottle in one hand and trying to steady himself on his wobbly feet with the other. Calling me a "dirty Jew" and "Christ-killer" along with other epithets, he slowly advanced toward me, waving the vodka bottle menacingly while staggering from side to side. I jumped up and kicked him with all my might in the middle of his body. The man looked at me in surprise, stood erect for a second and then fell over on his side with a thump, the remaining vodka soaking into his clothes. A few seconds later, the man was unconscious. If it hadn't been for his snoring, I would have been afraid that he was dead. I knew that it wouldn't be long before the station filled up, so I started walking toward Warsaw alongside the tracks.

When I arrived at the next station, it was beginning to fill up with passengers. At first I felt safe there, and unobserved since there were other children of my age. Seeing that they, however, were dressed up for the holiday and accompanied by their parents, I realized the danger of looking different from the other kids and being on my own. I started to feel as a hunted animal must when it is surrounded and knows that it is only a question of time before it is caught and killed.

At the back of the station, I came upon two filthy outhouse toilets and decided to hide there. I knew that no one from the festively dressed group of passengers would even dream of coming near these toilets. I went into one of the outhouses and locked the door, hoping that I would hear the whistle of the Warsaw-bound train when it arrived. As I stayed in the outhouse, I wondered how I could ask Mr. Serafinowicz for his help one more time; I wasn't worried that I was reaching the limits of his willingness to help me, but of his ability to.

These dark thoughts were interrupted by the sound of an approaching train, but the sound was not quite right – I could hear that the train wasn't going to stop and left my shelter to see what was happening. The stationmaster was trying to explain what was going on to a crowd of disappointed passengers: the German army command was apparently sending two trains full of Wehrmacht soldiers and equipment to fight the Jewish ghetto uprising. According to the telegram he had received, the second of these trains would be passing through shortly, to be followed by the regularly-scheduled passenger train.

The platform was now filled with a larger than normal number of travellers and, since I felt safer in a large crowd, I didn't return to my hiding place. The train to Warsaw didn't arrive for at least two hours, but the trip was short and uneventful and by midday I was back at Mr. Serafinowicz's apartment. I told him that although I sincerely appreciated all his previous help, I was unable to figure out what to do next. I think that it was Mrs. Serafinowicz who suggested that I go to a real village, inhabited by real farmers, and look for a job for the upcoming summer season.

The news was getting around that the ghetto insurgents were prepared to fight to the death and that the ghetto was going to be liquidated. The drunken janitor had hinted that he knew that Mr. Serafinowicz had been hiding Jewish kids and was trying to blackmail him even though it was no longer true. The janitor was hoping to receive further bribes despite knowing that smuggling in and out of the ghetto had ended.

We began to organize my escape from Warsaw once again. Mr. Serafinowicz told me that Piaseczno, a small town fifteen kilometres south of Warsaw, connected by a narrow-gauge railway, was surrounded by farms. Our plan was to buy a ticket that would take me even deeper into the middle of farm country than Piaseczno. To pose as a non-Jew among these farmers, Mrs. Serafinowicz warned me, it was absolutely necessary that I learn more Catholic greetings, and she made me memorize ones that she had tried to teach me earlier. We took our place in line at the train station and I gave Mr. Serafinowicz all the money I had. To our disappointment, the money would only buy me a ticket as far as Piaseczno, which wasn't our first choice since it was a town, rather than a village. Having no alternative, Mr. Serafinowicz made the decision for me and bought me the one-way ticket. He hadn't wanted to attract suspicion by making the people behind him wait while he consulted a child. As we shook hands, he wished me good luck and told me that in an emergency, I was always welcome at their apartment. I never did see him again.

Franciszek's Farm

Clutching the ticket that I hoped would at last take me to safety, I boarded the train. It departed on time and, momentarily forgetting my troubles, I enjoyed looking through the window at the passing countryside. We stopped once or twice at small stations to pick up other travellers. Then the conductor announced that the next stop would be Piaseczno – I remember well the nervous excitement that shook my body. My mouth was dry and I couldn't concentrate on the next stage of my plan; I had no one to count on but myself.

As I was getting off the train, I was almost knocked over by a unit of German soldiers, armed to the teeth, who were boarding the train heading back to Warsaw. I overheard the soldiers say that they were going to Warsaw to reinforce the German soldiers who were liquidating the ghetto. Some of them made comments that were, astonishingly, in praise of the Jews for standing up heroically to the Germans. These remarks were said in muted voices to avoid their being overheard by other Germans or their collaborators.

As had been true in Otwock, there were no farms in sight in Piaseczno, so I knew that I would have to leave the town as soon as possible. I didn't know the name of a nearby farming village to ask directions to and, what was worse, I didn't even know how to recognize a farming village. I finally decided to follow the railway tracks in the direction that would take me farther away from Warsaw.

Sooner or later, I felt, I would see a farm with cows, horses and other animals. After walking for what I thought was hours, I found myself surrounded by fields, trees and occasional rows of small houses with thatched roofs. I didn't see any animals near the houses, though, so I assumed that the real farms were still farther away.

It was almost dusk and I was just becoming afraid that I would have to spend the night outside when I spotted a tiny group of houses that looked more like a small town than a farming village. The sight of this little town made me feel hopeful and I decided to try my luck there so I left the train tracks and cut across the fields. My heart was beating wildly as I walked to the far end of the town, silently rehearsing my obligatory greeting. I don't know why I chose one house over another, but I found myself knocking at a door, trembling with fear.

A thin man opened the door and looked at me questioningly. I greeted him faultlessly and the standard reply came without hesitation. The smoothness of the ritual put me at ease and I began to tell a variation on my well-rehearsed story. The man seemed to be satisfied and invited me inside, asking me if I would like to eat something. I accepted gratefully and crossed myself before eating the piece of Easter cake he put in front of me.

After I had finished, he asked me about events in Warsaw. The fires were visible even at this distance and everyone who passed through told a different story about the ghetto uprising. Managing to sound detached (which was a miracle in itself), I gave him a version of these events that would not identify me as a sympathizer, much less as a Jew. After hearing me out, he asked me why I had come to the countryside. Without naming Mr. Serafinowicz, I told him that people in Warsaw had suggested that a young boy's best chance of finding a job in the summer season would be as a shepherd. The man told me that he couldn't employ me because he didn't have animals that needed tending, but that one of his relatives, Franciszek Puchała, lived nearby in the village of Runów. Franciszek, he said, was the richest farmer in the village, with thirty morguens (measures of land), six cows, two horses, chickens and pigs, and surely needed help for the summer. I felt better right away and later, when I lay down to sleep on a cot that my host had kindly made for me, I fantasized about riding horses and milking cows. The next morning, after having a breakfast of black bread with jam and a cup of black ersatz coffee with sugar, as I took my leave, my kind host said, "May you go with God," to which I replied, "Amen."

The morning was beautiful as I walked west along the train tracks. With every passing minute, the rising sun spread more warmth until I felt as if I were being wrapped in an invisible blanket. I saw small green leaves, harbingers of the approaching summer, and little creatures coming out of hibernation. Above my head, many different sizes and colours of birds were flying and singing to each other in a discordant yet beautiful symphony. I thought back to the wonderful summers I had spent at my grandmother's house in Tomaszów, with its lovely orchard and vegetable garden.

I was awoken from my reverie by changes on the horizon – in the distance were a group of thatched-roofed huts on either side of a sandy road. In the background, I could see a dense evergreen forest. The whole scene looked like one of the paintings I had seen on family visits to the museums in Warsaw. I forced myself back into reality as I entered the village and approached the first house. To my delight, the first and last names of the occupant were on the fence surrounding each hut, usually carved into a log.

When I found myself in front of the house of "A. Puchała," I stopped, not sure what to do – I was looking for Franciszek Puchała's name – but decided to go on rather than attracting suspicion in the middle of the village. I remembered that Franciszek Puchała was known as the richest farmer in the village, so I looked around for a house that might correspond to such wealth. I soon came to a spacious house with the name Franciszek Puchała painted on the fence. I saw two horses drinking from a trough, chickens noisily strutting around in the courtyard and could hear the grunting of a pig. I didn't see any cows – I later learned that when the cows were not in the pasture, they were chained up in the barn with containers of hay and plant cuttings.

Before I could knock on the door, a watchdog jumped out of his doghouse, barking at me menacingly. I froze, but fortunately the dog was stopped in his tracks at the end of his long chain. In response to my knock, the door was opened by a man who, as far as I could tell, looked like a typical farmer. After exchanging the required religious greetings, I launched into a condensed version of my story. When I finished, the man motioned for me to sit on a big bench against the wall. The room was without doubt the main one in the house – there was a long narrow table, with a bed on either side, and four or five chairs on which guests sat eating, drinking, smoking and talking in a kind of Polish that I could only partly understand. I listened intently to the conversation, trying to anticipate when I would have to start answering questions. The man whom everyone called Franciszek gave me a piece of cake and a large cup of ersatz coffee. I accepted the cake and coffee with sincere gratitude, crossed myself and said grace. Then it happened – I heard the word "Jew" several times in the conversation. I couldn't understand the exact context, but luckily they didn't pursue the subject. Not long after, people started to leave and I soon realized that the only people left were those who lived there. It seemed I had been given the job!

The mother, whose first name I never learned, must have been in her sixties and I realize now that she must have been in the early stages of dementia. She was a massive woman who spent most of her day in bed sleeping, or complaining and criticizing everyone around her. All through these tirades, she talked to herself, which is why everyone called her crazy. When her children asked her to do something specific such as peeling potatoes, she did it. But she refused to milk the cows.

Her eldest son, Wawżyniec, who had been sitting across from me talking to himself, suffered from a head injury he had gotten in World War I. Though harmless and willing to do anything asked of him, he never took any initiative in carrying out the many tasks required on the farm. Like his mother, he talked to himself constantly, telling himself stories, some of which made sense.

Franciszek, who was in charge of the farm, was next in age. He didn't smoke, drink or gamble, and I never saw him with women – he worked hard from sunrise to sunset. He had a highly developed sense of humour that he shared with everyone. I never heard religion discussed in his house, nor did I hear any of the Puchałas use any kind of profanity, unlike their neighbours. They all prayed before retiring for the night and crossed themselves before each meal. Franciszek went to church on most Sundays.

Next came Czesiek, a colourful character. His broken nose was the subject of many wild stories revolving around everything from differences of opinion to fights over women. He smoked and drank, though moderately. His Saturday nights were his great outlet. He would put on his best shirt, his knee-high leather boots and set out for a neighbouring village where young people gathered. Although he crossed himself before meals and prayed at night like the others, he did not attend Sunday mass as often as Franciszek or their sister, Helen.

Helen was the only daughter in the family. In my eyes, she was not as plain as many of the other peasant women; her features were delicate and complemented her expressive eyes, which she unconsciously used in every conversation. She had a great sense of humour and a remarkable voice that sometimes sounded arrogant and sometimes seemed to invite further conversation. She was curious and thirsty for knowledge, never too shy to encourage people whom she met – including me – to share what they knew with her. Like her brothers, she had barely finished elementary school, but she loved to read the newspapers that Franciszek brought home from the market. Helen was religious and went to mass every Sunday, dressed in her best clothes, a sight that must have turned the heads of all the village men. She loved organ music and admitted that it often brought tears to her eyes.

Helen was married to a farmer from the same village whose large family did not have an extra room for the couple, so the Puchałas allowed Helen and her husband to use a small bedroom off the kitchen at night. Since they were not able to live together, the anxious husband came over to the Puchała house regularly. He would spend a few minutes exchanging the news of the day with the Puchałas, then retire to the tiny bedroom to join Helen.

After the guests had left that first evening, the house returned to its regular rhythm. The old mother stretched out on the bed and began to snore loudly. After washing the dishes in a pail of warm water and putting the unfinished cake in the potato cellar, Helen and her husband retired to their bedroom. Wawżyniec was told to put out his cigarette and go to bed, which, in his and Czesiek's case, meant in the barn. Franciszek showed me the stable where he kept the cows and horses and the barn that was used to store wheat, grass, hay and flour. If he hired more people, he noted, the barn would become like a hotel.

When we got to what I realized was the toilet, Franciszek opened the door and told me to be careful not to fall in, especially at night. When I asked where the toilet paper was, he burst out laughing and, when he recovered his composure, told me that I had a whole stable full of hay and straw at my disposal. He assured me that I would get used to living conditions in the country very quickly. Finally, we arrived at the potato cellar that was to be my bedroom. Franciszek went into the house and came back with a plaid blanket and a farmer's sheepskin that was long enough to serve as a duvet. He wished me goodnight and said that he would wake me at 6:00 a.m.

I didn't feel at all sleepy, so, for the first time since my unplanned separation from my family, I began to relive every moment from the time I had said goodbye to my grandmother. I didn't want to think about the last time I had talked to my parents or sister. I also pushed away thoughts about when and how they might have died. I have continued this avoidance for most of my life.

Franciszek had left the tiny door to my potato cellar open, which allowed a little of the light from the bright, cloudless, star-filled sky to illuminate my quarters. My bed was a rectangular mound of hay and straw, raised about six inches off the floor, that was big enough to fit the blanket and sheepskin. I covered the hay with the blanket and lay on top of it fully dressed, pulling the sheepskin over me. Within a few minutes, I began to itch everywhere and I suddenly became afraid that creatures could enter through the open door. If I shut the door, I would be plunged into darkness, and I had always been afraid of the dark. Thankfully, I fell asleep much sooner than I imagined and the next thing I remember is Franciszek's voice waking me up.

Although it was only 6:00 a.m., the whole Puchała family was already up. Helen was busy at the stove and her brothers came and went, going between the house, the stable and the barn, letting the cows and horses out of the stable and steering them to their separate troughs. Helen took a basket full of grain out to the courtyard and fed the chickens and geese, imitating their calls as she did so. After all the animals were fed, everyone gathered in the house and ate their breakfast – a large piece of bread with a bit of jam on it, and black ersatz coffee. Franciszek said that it was still too cold to take the cows to the pasture, which was to be my job. In the meantime, I would be taught to perform many other tasks on the farm. Before we brought the cows and horses back to the stable, we would have to put new straw and hay in their stalls. He told me very seriously that animals performed their jobs better if they lived in clean surroundings.

Franciszek sent me to fetch a small pitchfork from the barn so he could teach me how to add hay and straw to the decomposing mass in the animals' stalls. The idea of work in the stalls, knee-deep in manure, made me nauseous. To make matters worse, everyone on the farm walked barefoot. Franciszek was understanding and assured me that I would only feel that way the first few times I did it. I took off my shoes and socks, which by this time were nothing but holes anyway, and jumped into the first stall. I didn't have to roll my pants up above my knees as the others did because I had fled the ghetto wearing shorts. As it turned out, the job wasn't all that unpleasant and, once I got used to the rank smell, I learned to perform it without any problem.

Franciszek and his siblings treated me like a member of the family, which made me more hopeful about my future. I liked them and felt grateful, but it was hard not to miss my own family and wonder what had happened to them. It was barely a week or ten days since the start of the ghetto uprising and, according to the news trickling in from Warsaw, the ghetto was still burning and its fighters were still keeping the German troops at bay. Thinking about the outcome and the fate of its possible survivors kept me from falling asleep at night.

One evening, a neighbour came and told us to go outside and watch the flames shooting up from the burning ghetto. As we joined a group of people excitedly pointing at the sight and talking about it, people began to dust off the ashes that had been carried all this way from the burning ghetto. I stooped to pick up a tiny piece of paper with burned edges and saw that it must have come from a Jewish book because the print was in Hebrew. I felt a physical pain and tears came to my eyes. Pretending I needed to go to the toilet, I ran to the outhouse, crumbled the scrap of paper and threw it away. I had to wipe the tears from my eyes before I could rejoin the group of onlookers. This was one of the worst moments during my stay at Franciszek's farm.

~

Over the next few days on the farm, I discovered that I was infested with lice. I tried to be inconspicuous in killing them with my nails, crushing them against walls but Helen noticed my fruitless battle. Being a straightforward and practical person, she told me to give her all my clothes, which she then boiled in hot water outside the house, then told Czesiek to shave my head with his straight razor. There was one problem, however – my only clothes were the ones on my back.

So I wouldn't have to go around in my birthday suit, Helen altered some old clothes of her brothers and she gave me a pair of pants from the boy next door, who was a relative. After several sessions of boiling my clothes and shaving my head, I was declared lice free. As a bonus, my wardrobe increased a little since some of my boiled clothes had survived.

Life on the farm was starting to get busier because of the approach of planting season. The trees were blooming in splendid, perfectly matched colours. Birds were flying from branch to branch, searching for the best place to build their nests and lay their eggs. Franciszek also began preparing me for the job I had been hired to do: being a shepherd. It had been a month or so since I had arrived and the whole village was busy preparing for the coming summer. Farmers were out in the fields, ploughing, fertilizing and seeding, and all around one could feel the controlled nervousness associated with the unpredictable outcome of their work. This mood seemed to be picked up by the animals as well. Cows were continually mooing in protest at being kept on chains in the stables, and were demanding to be taken to the pasture.

My day started when Czesiek woke me a little before sunrise. My first task was to unhook Blackie because, as the biggest and strongest cow, she was the undisputed leader. Happily, she would trot straight to the trough to drink, flipping her tail from side to side to chase the flies away, immediately followed by the other cows. Once I had directed the cows from the trough to the road leading to the pasture, I shut the double gate to the Puchała property to keep other animals out. With Blackie in the lead, and me behind the other cows, we walked to the pasture, where my only obligation was to ensure that the cows didn't stray. My biggest problem was fighting off sleep, which was ready to attack me at all times of the day.

A few hours later, Helen would bring me breakfast consisting of either potato soup with lots of vegetables and herbs or soup broth with bits of bacon. By the time breakfast arrived, I was starving and I can still remember how delicious it was. When Helen became pregnant and wasn't supposed to walk the half hour required to reach me, I ate half of a big piece of fresh, homemade, black bread with lard before I left the farm. I took the other half with me for a late morning snack in the pasture.

We used a common pasture for Runów and the surrounding villages, so I had the company of other shepherd boys. We did what other boys did in the countryside – pushing and shoving each other, telling tall tales and, later in the summer, swimming in the stream. In the fall, we made fires and roasted frogs, apples, potatoes and anything else edible that we could take from adjacent fields.

At the beginning of the summer, we wore cut-off pants in the water, but later, when the boys started swimming naked, I had two problems. The first was that I didn't know how to swim and the second was, of course, that I was worried about letting the other boys see me naked. I told them that I was from a very religious family, that it was against my beliefs to appear naked even in front of males, but that I would go in wearing my underpants. I also told them that I was willing to take swimming lessons from anyone who wanted to teach me. My explanation seemed to satisfy the boys. Although I was out of danger for the moment, I knew that this would not be the end of the story.

I was right to be worried. A few days later, another shepherd arrived who was older and taller than any of us. The day was hot and everyone went into the water. Fortunately, the new boy also went into the water with his pants on, telling the younger boys that they would understand why in a few years. Now there were two of us and the new boy was certainly stronger than all the other younger ones. To make him feel important – and hoping to change the subject – I challenged him to teach me how to swim. Part of me was scared silly to put my life in his hands, but another part of me actually wanted to learn to swim. The new boy accepted my challenge. He told me that further downstream, the descent from shallow to deep water was more gradual and was an ideal place to learn. He offered to carry me there on his back and with me on his back and the other boys yelling encouragement, we started our journey. To my shock, the water became deep immediately but I held on for dear life.

Terrified and with tears in my eyes, I begged the boy to go back, promising that I would try again the next day. Instead, he declared, "You'll learn now or never!" as he threw himself into the water and started to swim, dropping me like a bag of potatoes. I sank into water that was well above my head. When I somehow managed to come up for air, I felt my teacher's hands keeping my head out of the water. He ordered me to turn on my stomach and move my hands and feet, so I began to frantically slap the water and kick. To my astonishment, I heard applause and shouts of encouragement from the other boys. From then on, I took every opportunity to improve my swimming and learned very quickly. For the rest of the summer, my shepherd pals told the story to all newcomers and both my teacher and I were treated with more respect.

On the very hot summer days, I led the cows home at lunchtime for a break that lasted from about noon to two p.m., after which I took them back to the pasture. No one had watches; I learned how to tell time from the position of the sun, as the farmers did. One day, after putting the cows into their freshly cleaned stalls, I took a nap on one of the haystacks in the barn, as I always did after lunch.

As usual, Czesiek woke me up when it was time to go back to work. This time, however, instead of waking me and leaving the barn immediately, I heard him waiting at ground level near the door. This alarmed me and my mouth became dry. I slid down the haystack and walked toward the door, pretending that I found everything as usual. Chewing on a piece of straw, Czesiek demanded, "Show it to me." I felt a tremendous weight on my chest, but I didn't cry. Was it possible that my experiences in the past few months had built up my ability to feel horrendous pain inside without tears? I didn't obey the order but instead told Czesiek that I was Jewish. I don't know why I chose to admit that rather than do as I was told. After a moment, he almost gently told me to go to the house and ask Helen for bread and jam. I'm sure that this was Czesiek's way of comforting me. I had no idea who had found me out. It may have been that one of my shepherd companions had told his parents about my not wanting to swim in the nude and a naturally suspicious farmer had talked to Czesiek. After my confrontation with him, though, I was overwhelmed with insecurity and fear. It took a long time for me to feel safe again.

In the high summer I could see all around me the growing crops and other signs of nature taking its course. I was fascinated by the appearance of little calves and colts shadowing their mothers and trying without success to reach their teats. Unfortunately for the newborns, as soon as they could graze in the pasture, the mothers gradually withdrew from nursing and pushed the more aggressive ones away with a gentle nudge. I loved watching this young generation of animals frolicking, playing tug-of-war and sniffing everything they encountered for the first time.

One day during this pleasurable time, I was very surprised to see Helen running across the pasture toward me. My first thought was that she shouldn't be running because she was pregnant. When she reached me, trying to catch her breath and control her emotions, she looked around to make sure no one was near enough to overhear her. Putting her hand on my shoulder she said quietly, "The Germans are looking for Jews."

According to Helen, there were apparently two Jewish girls in an adjacent village who were, from what people were saying, paying for their upkeep with their bodies. Someone had denounced them to the Germans and they were now conducting a house-to-house, village-to-village search for other Jews. The Puchała family had heard about it from a peasant who was on his way to the market from one of the villages that had been searched. Helen and her brothers had decided to give me a chance to escape rather than just wait to see whether the Germans would find me. I was very frightened and couldn't focus on what I should do. Helen told me to run to the forest, gathering whatever fruit and vegetables I could find in passing, and hide there for two days. She would stay in the pasture with the cows and tell the neighbours that I had gone to the next village to help another farmer.

I took off immediately for the forest, crouching, zigzagging and hiding behind trees, bushes and the high wheat near its harvest time. In the end, I only stayed out one night. I decided to come home on the second evening when I saw German trucks filled with soldiers driving along the road toward Warsaw. I found out later that the two Jewish girls from the next village were the only victims of the hunt and that the German soldiers had taken them away.

Things settled down and preparations for the coming harvest were apparent on every farm. Franciszek started making hay to feed the animals in the winter and within a few days, the grass was beautifully preserved in tall cone-shaped haystacks. Next came the wheat harvest. With the exception of their mother, Franciszek's whole family took part, along with some hired help. I admired the planning, the preparations and the military precision with which everyone did their jobs. The men stood in a line, holding scythes that they swung from right to left in a semi-circle. The first man stepped forward three or four feet, at which point the man to his right started cutting the wheat a few feet behind. This relay carried on until the whole field was cut. They never missed a part of any row and when the field was cut, no plants remained standing.

The women waited until the last man was far away, then gathered and bundled the wheat, tying each bundle with loose straw, preparing them to be picked up the next day by a horse-drawn cart and taken to the stable for the separation of the grain from the chaff. My only function at this stage of the harvest was to help Helen with her part because of her pregnancy. Because there were so many other equally important things to do, the wheat harvest took place from noon to two p.m., during what was normally the long lunch break from the intense heat.

On one of these harvest days, I had brought the cows to the stable at noon as usual, but since the sky was clouding over, I decided to take the cows back to the pasture right away in case it rained. I started unchaining the cows, starting with Blackie, and it was only when I started walking toward the gate that I realized I had forgotten to open the double gate. I was supposed to do that before I started unchaining them; now only the small gate for people was open, so that only one cow could pass through at a time. At this rate, it took longer to get all six cows to get onto the road and instead of turning left toward the pasture as she always had, Blackie crossed the road and stuck one of her horns into a haystack that Franciszek had just built.

With her tail up in the air and head bent like a bull facing a matador, she ran around the haystack with one horn still attached. When I heard Franciszek yelling from the field, "Get her out of there!" I lunged at the out-of-control animal. Later, I compared myself to the Polish cavalry charging the German panzer tanks with lances in 1939. In both cases, the outcome was disastrous. Blackie now charged at me and with one horn threw me into the air. I fell on the opposite side of the road, right in front of the farmhouse. The next thing I remember is lying on Franciszek's bed with a terrible pain near my groin. Franciszek explained that Blackie had been momentarily blinded by the hay falling over her head and eyes, so I should have approached her from behind and hit her haunches with my stick.

I was very lucky. Although the wound was near my groin, it was not very deep – a layer of fat near the surface of my skin took the shock and there was little bleeding. Franciszek sent Czesiek for a nun at a nearby estate – where the nuns both ran the estate and also worked as teachers and nurses for the neighbouring farms – to dress my wound. I realized that in order to dress my wound, the nun would have to see what Czesiek had demanded to see a few weeks before. It was a scary moment.

The sister was covered from head to toe in a dark blue habit with rosary beads around her waist and a large crucifix around her neck. On her head she wore a snow-white headdress familiar to me from the nurses I had seen in Warsaw hospitals. In order to dress my wound, she asked me to remove my underpants, which I had rearranged a few moments before hoping to cover my circumcision. Struggling with the underpants, I looked at her and told her that if she would let me escape and not denounce me to the Germans, I would leave the village and join my friends in the forest. Although I had no such friends, I thought it might impress her and she might consider it safer to help me rather than turn me in.

She simply bent over me and, patting my forehead, said in a low voice, "Don't worry, child, I'll be back in a few days. Don't go anywhere." My next few days were filled with anxiety since I didn't wholeheartedly trust the nun. When she returned as promised, though, she declared my wound healed, changed the bandage for the last time and told me that I could go back to work. She made me promise to say five "Hail Marys." I jumped out of the bed, grabbed her hand and kissed it.

As the summer turned into the golden Polish autumn, the fields turned different colours as the crops that had grown there were harvested and stored in the farmers' barns. Some tree branches began to bend under the weight of maturing fruits and nuts. On the ground, one could see rabbits, groundhogs and other small, four-legged, furry animals scurrying about. They had been flushed out by the harvesting and by the fertilizing done in preparation for the next growing season. The days became shorter and cooler. At night, people closed their windows and one could see smoke coming out of chimneys, a sure sign that winter was approaching. Trees lost their multi-coloured leaves, falling into designs that could never be replicated in a man-made carpet.

The Puchała house became the unofficial gathering place for all the nearby farmers. They dropped by in the evenings to discuss everything from politics and gossip to problems with crops or animals, or just to share some homemade vodka. Sometimes one of the farmers would bring a Polish-language newspaper, heavily censored by the Germans, and try to unravel the truth from the lies. They would ask me to read aloud to them and explain the true meaning of what was printed there. I finally began to understand what my father had meant when he told me that you have to learn to read between the lines.

From time to time, we received visits from the guerrilla units of the Polish underground army that were stationed in the nearby forest. The units were composed of men and women who had escaped from the Nazis, who would have sent them to Germany as slave labour or to a concentration camp. The visits lasted only a few hours and the time was spent mostly in feeding them, letting them bathe or wash in the same wooden tub that was used for laundry and for the weekly bath of each person on the farm, and giving privacy to a few couples for their intimate relations.

Neighbouring farmers brought food to the Puchała house for the partisans. They were very careful about what they brought, since all the animals were registered by the Germans, who also counted the number of litres of milk and kilos of potatoes that each farmer had to hand over to them each week. If two calves were born instead of one but only one was registered, for example, it was safe to give one of the calves to the guerrilla fighters. Occasionally, the partisans paid for what they received out of money they had stolen from the Germans or that had been dropped for them from Soviet or English planes. They also brought something even more welcome – leaflets that contradicted the Polish newspapers that were subject to German censorship.

I particularly remember one of the partisans' last visits, toward the end of my season on the farm. The officers in the group told us that the Red Army, which included Polish units, was approaching the Polish border and that the end was in sight. It was inspiring to see men and women of different ages and backgrounds among the partisans. Although they were dressed in civilian clothes, each fighter had a few items that identified him or her as a soldier. They wore high boots, into which they tucked their pants; the women among them wore pants instead of skirts. Everyone had wide military belts with a variety of items attached that could be used in battle – bayonets, hand grenades and cartridges full of bullets for both handguns and rifles.

The partisans also wore wide armbands of red and white, the colours of the Polish flag, with two or three initials printed on them, abbreviations of the name of the political party to which the fighter belonged. For example, AK signified Armia Krajowa (Home Army) and PPR signified Polska Partia Robotnicza (Polish Workers' Party). Although each group tried to maintain ideological homogeneity, it was not always possible and the various partisan groups generally cooperated with each other despite differences in their political beliefs. They usually only stayed on the farm for one day and one night. During their stay, heavily armed guards were stationed at each entrance to the village and two men were also posted near the railway station in case the Germans arrived by train rather than by truck.

I became aware of a change in the mood among the farmers. A few months before, they hadn't been sure that the end of the war was near. Now, they were interpreting all sorts of small incidents as indicators that the Germans were about to retreat. When they went to markets in Warsaw, for example, they saw an increase in westbound trains transporting wounded soldiers and military equipment from the eastern front. Some of the buildings in Warsaw that had been occupied from the beginning of the war by different branches of the German administration were being vacated and closed. As for the propaganda machine, the caricatures of the Jews alone had given way to a combination of caricatures of Soviets and Jews. Now the Jews were supposedly directing the Soviet soldiers in a joint effort to eliminate the Polish race.

One fall day, Franciszek told me that he would be going to

Piaseczno shortly to buy winter necessities for the family and farm. He said that I had earned some money during my stay on the farm and wanted to know what he could buy me for the coming winter. He also told me that there were too many people registered on his farm and that the Germans would surely take one or two to slave labour in Germany. Since I was too young, his mother too old and sick, and one of his brothers mentally handicapped, the victims would be Helen, Czesiek or himself. He broke the news that I should go back to Warsaw, stay there until the following spring and come back for next year's season. Seeing the tears in my eyes, he said that I still had a few weeks to make plans for my departure and we decided on the purchases he would make for me: a new pair of boots and a pack of 100 Mewa brand cigarettes that were very popular in Warsaw.

The boots that Franciszek bought me were the only kind I could afford – ankle-high with inflexible wooden soles nailed to a type of ersatz leather that was no thicker than paper. When I tried them on I almost fell down because I couldn't bend my feet. Finally, however, I figured out how to slide rather than walk in them. The 100 Mewa cigarettes came in a package that reminded me of my smuggling days in the ghetto.

The night before my departure I concentrated on forming a survival plan. Although there had been scary moments on the farm, I knew that in Warsaw I wouldn't be able to reproduce the safety I had experienced there. My priorities were finding a place to stay at night, something to do during the day and food. I remembered reading in the newspaper that homeless people spent the night in bombed-out buildings during the winter, keeping themselves warm with newspapers and rags. During the day, I could join dozens of other boys and girls selling cigarettes. Food I would steal from the stores, markets and garbage cans. I understood very well that you had to buy cheaper than you sold in order to make money, but I wouldn't be able to sell the cigarettes at a profit because I had bought them retail. My main purpose in selling cigarettes would be to blend in with the other street vendors.

On the appointed day, Franciszek and I walked through the forest to the train station eating newly ripened berries. We soon heard the whistle of the approaching train and shook hands. Sliding along in my wooden shoes, my feet covered with rags that Helen had given me instead of socks, I climbed up the stairs of the train. A few minutes later, Franciszek, Runów and the forest were out of sight.

Return to Warsaw

As a ticket-carrying passenger I was allowed to sit in one of the many empty seats in the train cars, but I preferred to remain standing on the enclosed platform. I was afraid that sitting alone without an adult would attract attention. As I stood looking out the window during the hour-long train ride to Warsaw, all sorts of thoughts passed through my mind. I was feeling sorry for myself, a feeling I did my best to suppress as counterproductive. I realized that indulging in self-pity was a way to avoid preparing to survive in Warsaw. Instead, I tried to remember the names of people I could safely approach to ask for help. Out of nowhere, the horrific scene of the Jewish woman standing on the roof of a burning building during the ghetto uprising appeared in my mind. Again, I saw her step onto the edge of the roof and jump down into the flames.

Shaken, I re-focused on the view outside the train and the terrible vision receded. I now knew what I was going to do when I reached Warsaw – the incident had brought Mr. Serafinowicz and his family into the forefront of my mind. I decided that since he was the one who had directed me to the relative safety of the countryside, I could now ask for his help again. In fact, I saw no other choice.

Half an hour after arriving in Warsaw, I arrived at Mr. Serafinowicz's familiar apartment just outside the brushmakers' ghetto. To my horror, I saw that the ghetto had been systematically destroyed, house by house. It was impossible that anyone had survived there. As I stared at the ruins, a terrible thought went through my mind: what had happened to the larger ghetto, where my family had been? I was afraid that their fate had been the same as that of the inhabitants of the small ghetto.

I knocked at the door of Mr. Serafinowicz's apartment and when the door opened, Mrs. Serafinowicz quickly pulled me inside. Not having eaten since early that morning, I greedily gobbled up the tea and sandwich that she offered me. Only then did I realize that Mr. Serafinowicz was not there. The three children suddenly appeared and cuddled up to their mother. I stopped eating and, looking into Mrs. Serafinowicz's tear-filled eyes, asked where he was. In a voice that I could barely hear, she told me that Mr. Serafinowicz had been caught in an unexpected street raid. The few surviving witnesses had told her that her husband had tried to escape into an alley but unfortunately slipped and fell. Two German soldiers tried to force him to get up, but when he motioned that he couldn't stand, one of the soldiers had, without hesitation, shot him dead.

This atrocity had taken place a few months earlier. Wiping her eyes and reaching across the table to take my hand, Mrs. Serafinowicz said that she was not the only victim of these cruel times in Poland. She asked where I had been and what I had been doing during the six months or so since Mr. Serafinowicz had taken me to the train station. I briefly recounted my story, ending with the plea for help that I had wanted to make to her husband. I explained that I didn't know anyone in Warsaw other than her, that I had no money and that I couldn't go back to Runów. Mrs. Serafinowicz replied that there was no way for her to hide me in her apartment without the drunken janitor finding out. She added that she herself had no money and was on social assistance.

Mrs. Serafinowicz asked if I remembered any Polish people who had either worked for my mother or knew my father through business. As quick as a lightning bolt, I remembered two different conversations with my father. The first was when he gave me the birth certificate of Piotr Grodzieński, which he had bought from our neighbour who had worked for the Grodzieński family before they were sent to a concentration camp for political reasons. In the second conversation, my father had told me about a Mr. Targonski, the owner of Opus, our competitor in the dry cleaning business. Until the closure of the ghetto, they had maintained their friendship despite being competitors. When the Germans began confiscating Jewish valuables, my father had given Mr. Targonski three items for safekeeping: a silver cigarette case, with a beautiful sapphire forming the torso of the spider design; a fountain pen of the highest quality that, matching the cigarette case, was enveloped in a gold spider web with another spider and sapphire on it; and a signet ring bearing the same spider design as the cigarette case and fountain pen. The top of the ring opened to reveal a tiny photo of our family. My father had told me that if I was ever in need of any help or advice, I should speak to Targonski personally and tell him that I was the son of Jerzy Ney.

I had no idea where to find this man, but Mrs. Serafinowicz said that Opus was a well-known dry cleaning company with several branches in Warsaw, one of which was in her neighbourhood. By going to the local branch, I could find out the address of Mr. Targonski's office. I offered Mrs. Serafinowicz my condolences again, kissed her hand, hugged each of the children and said goodbye.

As I walked in my uncomfortable shoes, I was cold through and through. I had no winter coat and it was a windy November day. When I went inside the Opus shop, I approached the clerk and, trying to sound both nonchalant and authoritative, I asked, "Will you please tell me where I can find Mr. Targonski?" The clerk looked shocked at this request from a shabby-looking boy, but my knowing the name Targonski obviously impressed her. She said that she didn't know where he was at the moment, but gave me directions to the main office of Opus. When I arrived there, it was already quite dark and the snow was falling thick and fast. To my horror, I saw a guardhouse in front of the building with an armed German soldier. It was too late to turn back; I knew that if I did the soldier would stop and interrogate me. Waving the paper with the address above my head, I advanced toward the guard, exclaiming in the most normal voice I could muster, "Pan [Mr.] Targonski! Pan Targonski!"

The guard ushered me through the open gate and I soon found myself on the ground floor of the two-storey building. Climbing the stairs, I knocked on the only door and, hearing the command to enter, walked into an office filled with men and women who were standing around drinking. The room fell silent. When one of the men asked me what I wanted, I said that I had to talk to Mr. Targonski in private. Another man motioned for me to follow him. We went to an empty room, where he said coldly, "I am Targonski. What do you want?" "I am the son of Jerzy Ney," I replied. Without saying a word, he grabbed me by the collar and pushed me through the doors and down the stairs. I felt like sitting down on the floor and crying, but I remembered the armed guard outside. Something inside me revolted against my apparent fate and I marched out of the building, past the guard, and set off into the darkness.

Large, heavy snowflakes were falling and unlike the earlier snow that had melted on the ground, it formed a soft, white layer on the pavement, a harbinger of the coming winter. I had no idea what to do next and started to cry. After a few minutes, a woman wrapped in a heavy plaid shawl appeared on the deserted street and asked me what was wrong. I told her that I had no place to go. She took off her shawl and gave it to me, saying apologetically, "Child, I cannot take you with me, but this will keep you warm." As she started to leave, she gave me directions to a religious institution where homeless people could find shelter at night. She said that it was too far to walk and took a tram ticket out of her purse. With a heartfelt, "May God repay you," I headed toward the streetcar stop a few feet away, holding the folded shawl under my arm. Wearing a woman's shawl would have attracted too much attention.

When my tram arrived, I went inside the car rather than staying on the platform because of the cold weather. The only other passenger was a woman who was sitting a few seats from me. She stared at me, probably because of the oddness of my appearance and the fact that a child would not normally be alone there at that time of night. She suddenly jumped up and on her way to the door, stopped in front of me and said in an outraged voice, "Child, lice are crawling on you!" She hurried off the tram as soon as it stopped. I no longer cared whether I lived or died; I was frozen, hungry and at a total loss.

When I arrived at the shelter a few moments later, I stood in front of an odd-looking man sitting at a desk. He had a large crucifix hanging around his neck but wasn't dressed like a priest and didn't look like a civilian either. Later, I learned that the shelter was run by a religious order of men who were not priests but brothers, a vocation unknown to me at the time. The shelter was frequented by the poorest homeless, many of them from cities and towns outside Warsaw. Among them were petty criminals and *Volksdeutsche* deserters from the German army. In short, these were the most unfortunate and desperate people searching for a night's shelter where they would be warm enough to survive. The man behind the desk didn't ask my name, nor did he demand any identification papers. He could tell that I fit in perfectly with the shelter's population. He told me where to find my bunk bed and that there was a toilet at each end of the hall, warning me that I mustn't make it any dirtier than it already was. He added that there would be a blanket on the bunk that I had to leave there when I left the following morning.

I thanked him and walked toward the room. I was beginning to feel warm thanks to the wood-burning stoves on each floor of the building. Unlike most bunk beds, this one had no lower bunk, which was reassuring since I would have no one near me. The adjacent bunk was occupied by two young boys who were playing cards and paid no attention to me. A man came into the room to collect money from everyone, claiming that it was for wood. I gave him a few złotys, which, to my relief, he accepted without further ado. I overheard a few people discussing this money collector, saying that he was a deserter from a unit of the German military made up of non-German volunteers.

Then another religious brother came into the room, clapped several times and waited for the noise to subside. When he began reciting the Lord's Prayer in Polish I joined in enthusiastically, hands folded in the prayer position, looking like a little saint and counting my blessings that Helen had taught me the prayer. At the end, the brother added a few lines of homemade requests and petitions, then ordered lights out and complete silence under penalty of being expelled from the shelter. A few minutes later, the electric light went off and the only remaining light was the glow of the wood stove. It was an eerie scene because I could only see moving shadows busily arranging their blankets and turning from one side to another. I pulled the blanket over my head and fell sound asleep.

I was awakened the next morning by the sound of clapping from the same brother as last night who repeated the previous night's prayer ritual. My two young neighbours and I were sitting on our bunk beds facing each other with our legs dangling and I saw one of the boys whisper something in his friend's ear. The way he looked at me made me feel that somehow he had discovered my secret. I continued to pray with the others, but with one hand began to scratch my body all over and discreetly check the condition of my fly buttons. They were all closed. At the end of the prayer, as we all made the sign of the cross, the boy elbowed his comrade and pointed at me. He then made an extra sign of the cross while whispering in his friend's ear. When the brother left and I got ready to leave the shelter, the older boy blocked my way, telling me to wait a moment and ordered his younger companion to fetch their uncle.

I began to feel desperate. To my surprise, the "uncle" turned out to be the same man who had collected money the night before. This time, however, he asked me in German for my papers. I began to relax since I was carrying the baptismal certificate of a Christian boy. Looking at the document for a few seconds, the "uncle" uttered the much-desired "Alles in Ordnung" (Everything is in order) and said that I was free to go. This was the only time that I asked God to bless the Germans for their love of *Papiere* (documents). Although he was Polish rather than German, the "uncle" was trying to imitate the German officers whom he had seen inspecting people's papers and deciding their fate on the basis of them. I didn't wait another second, and dashed out the door and down the steps. I was back in the same situation I had been in the night before – I was out in the cold with nothing to eat and nowhere to go.

It had stopped snowing and somehow I no longer felt as cold as I had the previous night. I walked aimlessly, not knowing how to spend the day, until I remembered my plan to sell cigarettes on the street. Although I didn't yet know where I could spend the nights, I could start with selling the cigarettes. I was counting on my ragged, dirty and skinny appearance encouraging people to help me by buying my wares.

I went to the famous Marszałkowska Street, where I was heartened to see many people and open shops with simple but beautiful displays in preparation for the approaching holiday season. I stopped at a corner and took the box that contained 100 Mewa cigarettes out of my knapsack. Filled with trepidation, I took a deep breath and began to call out the same mantra used by all street cigarette vendors, whether in the ghetto or outside, Jewish or not, to glamorize their brand: "Mewy! Mewy! Papierosy, extra płaskie! Papierosy! Mewy! Mewy!" (Mewy! Mewy! Cigarettes, extra smooth! Cigarettes! Mewy!) I tried desperately to sound like the other cigarette-vendor boys.

For the first time, I experienced how it feels to fail in business. After yelling at the top of my lungs for about ten minutes, I was already hoarse and not only had I not sold a single cigarette, no one had even stopped to ask the price. Then I noticed a group of about ten young boys, all cigarette or newspaper vendors, marching toward

me at a fast clip, shouting. Every second word was an antisemitic slur.
I quickly put away my cigarette box and jumped onto a passing tram
– I knew that I couldn't fight off ten boys at once. I jumped off the
tram as soon as I thought I was safe, not wanting to find myself in an
unfamiliar part of Warsaw. The day was now already almost over and
I couldn't tell whether I was more tormented by cold or hunger. All
my bravura was dissolving into deep depression.

I had overheard two people talking about a social welfare organization that sheltered the homeless and since it wasn't far from
where I had jumped off the tram, I decided to go there. Rada Główna
Opiekuńcza (RGO, Main Welfare Council) was a non-religious organization that had existed long before the war. It had helped thousands
of people and, most important, was tolerated by the Germans, probably because they could always "recruit" slave labourers there.

The RGO shelter was divided into two sections, one for men and
one for women. The men's section consisted of two large rooms, with
a sawdust-burning stove in the centre of one. A series of pipes led
along the walls from the stove into the other dormitory. In place of
bunk beds were military stretchers. People could shower in makeshift
washrooms in the long corridor outside the rooms, but they were not
allowed to loiter on the premises, nor could they cook or prepare
food. These rules were not strictly applied but the management expected occupants to keep the rooms clean. The distribution of cleaning tasks, however, was left in the hands of the occupants.

The man who explained these rules to me when I arrived added
that we were expected to only use the premises at night. To my relief,
this rule was not enforced and I was able to spend most of my time in
the dormitory, leaving only when necessary to steal food or make a
little money carrying luggage or packages, mostly for women. I could
only stay at the shelter for a few days, so I still had to find a way to
survive in the longer term.

Early in the morning of my fourth or fifth day at the shelter, everyone in the men's dormitories was surprised by the arrival of a German

Wehrmacht officer, followed by one of the shelter managers and a man in a wheelchair. The German officer said something to the shelter manager, who informed us in Polish that there would be a medical exam under the observation of the German officer. All the healthy men would be sent to labour camps in Germany. He added that we shouldn't be nervous because we were not being arrested, nor treated as criminals; we would be joining many other men and women from the occupied countries who were already working in Germany under conditions inspected by the Red Cross. He told us to form a line, which was so long that it ran in and out of both dormitories and ended at the closed door of a third room. The man in the wheelchair, also a Pole, introduced himself as the doctor who would perform the medical exam and made an effort to calm us. He promised to answer all our questions after the examination. The officer and the doctor went to the third room, which would serve as the examination room, and shut the door, while the manager organized the lineup.

The examinations began and the men went in and out, one at a time, every few minutes. I managed to worm my way to the end of the line and desperately tried to hear the exchanges between the men waiting near the door and those coming out. I heard what I needed to know – one man came out of the exam room laughing and said that the whole "examination" consisted of an inspection of his penis. Trying not to show my panic, I looked for an escape route or hiding place, but there were none. To make matters worse, two or three armed German soldiers stood in the only doorway leading out to the street. The memory of the *Umschlagplatz* incident left my mouth dry and I wet my pants.

My turn arrived and I went through the door. To my left was the German officer, looking out a huge floor-to-ceiling window onto the street, his hands clasped behind his back. The paraplegic doctor sat behind a large desk writing something and, when he finished, he lifted his head and asked impatiently what I was waiting for. Without turning toward us, the German officer said, "Was ist los?" (What's going on?) I opened my fly and showed the doctor what he needed to see. To my surprise, the doctor said, "Alles in Ordnung," all the while shooting daggers at me. He motioned to me to close my fly and told me to go back to the dormitory and wait for him. Quietly, he hissed, "Don't do anything stupid." The inspection ended and the German officer left the dormitory followed by the two soldiers. A huge truck was parked outside the building and the men chosen for slave labour in Germany began taking their places in the back of it.

I waited impatiently for the doctor to reappear, thinking that these could be my last moments on earth. The fact that the German officer had left without dealing with me was reassuring, but I nevertheless began to imagine the tortures that the doctor might inflict on me. He was the only person who knew my secret. When at last the door opened and the doctor wheeled his chair toward me, I could see that he was furious. He told me that I had been stupid and irresponsible and could have gotten everyone killed. Eventually, he calmed down and told me that my age had saved me from deportation, but I was not too young to die. Near the end of his tirade his tone softened and he asked where my parents were and where I had lived before coming to the shelter. I related my history and included my recent encounter with Targonski as a tactic to gain his sympathy, to make him feel guilty enough to help me.

Following our discussion, the doctor asked me to push him out to the street and gave me directions to the office of an organization that placed young war victims in institutions. He assured me that they would be able to find me a safe place. We arrived at the office about a quarter of an hour later and the doctor disappeared into an office to speak to a man he obviously knew. When they emerged not long after, the doctor told me that the organization already had a place in mind for me – an institution run by Roman Catholic priests of the Salesian order. The doctor then said goodbye and left.

I was next interviewed by several men and women. To my surprise, I felt quite secure with them. Perhaps it was the gentle way they questioned me. They asked me whether I had any identification papers and were pleasantly surprised when I pulled out the baptismal certificate of Piotr Grodzieński issued by the diocese of Warsaw. When they asked what had happened to my parents, I told them that they had been taken from our house in Warsaw by the Gestapo while I was in eastern Poland with relatives and that it was impossible for me to get back there. After the interview, a young woman told me to take a shower and showed me where to find the bathroom. When I returned half an hour later, I could tell that something was wrong. The man, whom I took to be the director, had my baptismal certificate in his hand. He asked me which of my parents was Jewish; I felt the earth open beneath my feet.

Seeing my shock, the director explained, "My dear Piotr, while you were being interviewed, one of my secretaries went to the address on the certificate. The building where your parents lived is ten minutes from here and a janitor who has worked there for years is still there. He confirmed that your parents were taken away and have never come back. He also said that he didn't know where you were and has had no further contact with the family. He told my secretary which one of your parents was Jewish and now you must tell me which one."

I was confused. The family name Grodzieński was not Jewish and if my father had known that Mrs. Grodzieńska was Jewish, he would never have bought the baptismal certificate. Thinking it through at the speed of light, I answered as calmly as I could, "My mother." To my great relief, my judge and jury exchanged satisfied looks. The director said gently that they were sorry that I had been left an orphan. "If you agree," he continued, "we can place you in an institution for boys and girls in similar situations. It is run by lay people and priests of the Salesian order, founded in Italy by St. John Bosco."

I thanked them fervently, hoping they understood that I knew they were risking their lives for me. The director handed my file to one of the women, telling her where to take me and what to say when we arrived. He wrapped both hands around mine and said, "May God bless you and take care of you," to which I answered, "Amen." I wasn't even sure if it was appropriate or not. I shook hands with everyone, grabbed my knapsack with its still unopened box of cigarettes and followed the young woman out the door.

While we were walking, the woman told me a bit about the life awaiting me at the institution, including the fact that any money or valuables I had (in my case, the box of cigarettes and a few złotys) would be taken away and kept until I left. If I wanted to leave them with her instead, she told me, she could use them to bring me things I might need. I had no reason to doubt what she said, yet I had no reason to believe that I would ever see her again, whether I gave her any valuables or not. From my experience as a smuggler, where paying bribes was a daily necessity, I knew she was playing the role of the Polish goons outside the ghetto and I was better off playing her game. I told her that I had no money or valuables but would be happy if she would take my cigarettes and, in exchange, bring me something from time to time. She assured me that she would do so. I thanked her warmly, knowing that I would likely never see her again.

We soon arrived at a three-floor apartment building. My escort rang the bell and a man who looked through the peephole let us in. In the director's office, a man introduced himself as Mr. Kapusta, shook my hand and asked me my name. My escort handed over my file and asked me to wait outside the office for a few moments. She must have told Mr. Kapusta that my mother was Jewish, for it was clear afterward that he knew. After I came back into the room, she kissed me lightly on the head, promised to visit and reassured me that I would be well taken care of.

A New Beginning

I was to find out much later that the man I knew as Jan Kapusta was an ordained priest whose scholarly specialty was biblical Hebrew. He had spent many years in Palestine and was internationally known for his studies of the Bible and for his work as a university lecturer and theologian. He was wanted by the Germans because of his renown in a discipline that associated him with Jewish scholars. I was always to address him as Pan Dyrektorze (Mr. Director), but the only way I can comfortably speak of him now is under his *nom de guerre*, Pan Jan Kapusta.

Pan Kapusta told me about the institution, including the rules and regulations that were to be obeyed under punishment of caning. I would be placed in a group of boys headed by a prefect, a boy usually older than the others. Each group had its own dormitory and dining room table in the refectory, where we would also study and do our homework. He warned me not to start fights and to stay away from the girls' side of the institution, which was in an adjacent building. Finally, Pan Kapusta assured me that I would be welcome to see him any time. He then took me to meet my prefect, whose job, besides enforcing discipline, allowed him extra privileges. It didn't take long for me to find out what this meant.

The prefect was tall, slender and bespectacled, with his hair cropped in military fashion, as was *de rigueur* for all the boys in the institution. He had an intelligent-looking face and piercing eyes that seemed to be constantly searching for something. He motioned for me to follow him, saying that he would start the tour with the sleeping quarters. This is where I got my first lesson on the privileges of prefects. He shared his relatively large bedroom with only one other boy and had a balcony with a view of the recreation yard, whereas I would share mine with five others, and the six of us had only one tiny window that looked out on a small courtyard.

The washroom consisted of a few sinks and shower stalls – the toilets were in a separate, adjacent room – and these facilities served all fifty or sixty boys in the institution. Several large rooms on the second floor served as classrooms for both boys and girls. A large room on the same floor had been converted into a chapel, with an altar with religious objects placed on a plain white cloth. A vigil light, a candle in a red glass container, hung from the ceiling behind the altar. I also noticed a compartment that turned out to be a confessional. We didn't go inside the chapel, but stood in the open doorway, where the prefect crossed himself. Since my near-catastrophe in the first Warsaw shelter, not only did I cross myself, but I also genuflected.

On the ground floor was the refectory, a huge room with many wooden tables. Instead of chairs, there were benches, except at the head of the table, where the prefect had the privilege of a chair. The building occupied by the girls was adjacent to ours in the same courtyard, and the only facility that we shared was the refectory. We all ate at the same time at opposite sides of the hall. Since there was never a great deal to eat, the time in the dining room was brief.

The prefect and I went back to the third floor, where he told me that I would be given a uniform, an ankle-length nightshirt and a haircut. I was to shower and, since it was already evening, return to my assigned bed. Although only one boy was allowed in a shower stall at a time, taking a shower still presented a risk – after the shower, we had to come out of the stall naked to dry ourselves and give the shower space to the next boy. I quickly learned to manipulate the soap in such a way that my penis was always covered; after I got out, I manipulated the towel to hide my private parts.

Fortunately, the showering problem was eliminated a few days later. The director told the prefect that I was to shower alone to avoid indecent questions from the younger boys. According to the prefect, this was for religious reasons – he said that he also showered separately because Mother Nature had already endowed him with developing private parts that the young boys should not see. This arrangement also gave him more time to supervise activities in the washroom and dormitory.

In bed that night, I thought about my family for the first time in many weeks. I saw their faces in front of me and heard their voices. This time, I didn't see them dead or being killed. In my mind, it was only a question of time until we were reunited, even though the ghetto had been destroyed. I accepted the fact that my elderly grandmother must have died, but surely my young, pretty sister would survive, even in a concentration camp. She could have been rescued by a German officer who wanted her to be his mistress. She didn't look or sound Jewish; she had green eyes, often dyed her hair with peroxide, spoke no Yiddish and her Polish was flawless, without any trace of a Jewish accent.

On the morning of my first full day, I entered into the institution's regular routine. We gathered in the refectory around 8:00 a.m. for the standard breakfast of a large slice of bread smeared with jam and a cup of ersatz coffee with saccharine. After the meal was served, the prefect motioned to us to stand up for a brief prayer and then he wished us, "Smacznego!" (Bon appétit!)

To my great surprise, no one except me started to eat when we sat down. The other boys looked at me angrily, so I put down my bread, trying to figure out what I was supposed to do. It became clear a few seconds later. The prefect took his spoon and dug out all the bread inside the heel of the loaf – larger than the slice that the rest of us received – and passed what was now a hollowed-out container to the boy on his right. That boy then scraped all his jam into the hollowed heel and passed it along to the next boy. Each boy in turn put all his own jam into the prefect's bread until it had returned to its owner. I had no choice but to follow suit. This injustice scandalized me and the fact that I couldn't do anything about it was frustrating.

After breakfast, we went to our assigned classrooms, which were mixed with boys and girls as well as with different ages and levels of knowledge. On the basis of minimal testing, I was assigned to Grade 6, although I had only finished Grades 1 and 2 before the war. I was now almost thirteen and a half. Our subjects were reading and writing in Polish, arithmetic and the Catholic religion. History, geography and the sciences were excluded out of fear that the German authorities might close the institution if they disapproved of the course content.

The school day lasted through the morning and the beginning of the afternoon, with the rest of the afternoon spent on homework and on free time or recreation activities. On Sundays and religious holidays the boys and girls attended mass, during which many of them took communion. A few weeks passed uneventfully, and I fully blended into my new life. I found the lessons interesting and well presented and felt that the teachers sincerely tried to eliminate the educational gaps among their pupils. They often did individual tutoring during recreation periods. Thanks to this improvised school, I finished Grade 6 in 1943 with average results.

Pan Kapusta was not our regular classroom teacher, but gave occasional lectures on diverse topics that were mostly based on his personal experiences. Well educated and well travelled, his talks usually involved religion and his travels in distant lands, especially Palestine. He spoke Hebrew fluently. I was saddened to learn years later that he had died during the Warsaw Uprising, struck by a bomb that hit the building he was in. This was ironic because I remembered a beautiful summer day when, while Pan Kapusta was playing ball with us – a special occasion in itself – one of the boys asked him to explain what happened when a bomb fell directly on someone. The eastern front was already in Poland and, although it was hard to get reliable information, there were rumours that the Red Army was approaching Warsaw. The Soviet air force was flying over Warsaw toward Berlin every day and, although they weren't bombing Warsaw, we all descended into the basements, transformed into bomb shelters, during the raids.

Pan Kapusta decided his answer should be heard by all the pupils, so he gathered us around him and said that when people in bomb shelters hear the blood-curdling whistle of bombs flying through the air, they are paralyzed with fear, certain the bombs will fall on them. In reality, however, the people who are directly hit do not hear the bombs at all, and have no time to experience any fear. Most died very quickly. As fate would have it, Pan Kapusta's death was an example of a direct hit.

~

The peace and quiet at the institution was not to last forever. A few weeks after I arrived, I showered immediately after the prefect and then, on my way to the dormitory, passed the open door of his room. I suppose he had left the door open to show the younger boys his constant vigilance. He was sitting on his bed clipping his toenails, with his legs bent in such a way that his nightshirt was gathered around his thighs. This position gave me a full view of his genitals and, just as I was passing, he lifted his head and our eyes met. We were both horrified because it was clearly evident that he was circumcised. The prefect jumped up, grabbed my arm, pulled me inside his room and shut the door. Still holding me, he put his other hand around my neck and started squeezing, hissing, "You son of a bitch, one word to anyone and I'll throw you out the window!" He opened the door of his room and pushed me into the corridor.

That night, I lay awake for a long time. All sorts of scenarios passed through my mind as I desperately tried to make sense of this threatening confrontation. If there were two Jewish boys here, maybe there were others as well. Assuming for the moment that there were, was this how the others would react? I would have to discover who they were in order to protect myself. How were they managing to hide themselves? I assumed that the director had allowed me to shower alone so I wouldn't be discovered. This meant that I had one powerful ally, but I couldn't be sure that the same was true of the other adults on staff.

The rest of 1943 went by without any further incidents. We weren't given any news about events in the outside world. Polish newspapers were still being thoroughly censored and although there were a few Polish underground papers, it was forbidden to possess them, under penalty of death. All the radios had been confiscated at the beginning of the war, but everyone knew someone who knew someone with a hidden radio. The ones that were worth their weight in gold were the shortwave radios, but no one in the institution dared have one. The only legitimate medium that circulated news freely was the "agency" known as Jedna Pani Powiedział (JPP), meaning "one woman said" – that is, word-of-mouth rumours.

I was most interested in news from the eastern front. We knew that the German army was in retreat and that the mighty Soviet army, equipped by the United States, was advancing steadily westward through Poland toward Germany. In Warsaw, two underground political movements were prominent and, although their ideologies were opposed, they were united in their strategic planning and continuous acts of sabotage. The right-wing of the Polish underground was represented mainly by the Armia Krajowa. There were a few right-wing parties that never won any great following and disappeared after the war. There was also a Polish organization in Moscow made up of members of the Polish intelligentsia, army officers and ordinary soldiers, who had all been captured by the Soviets during their invasion of eastern Poland in 1939. The Polish government-in-exile in London was more widely recognized internationally, in particular by the US and its allies. Aligned with them were members of the Polish military who had escaped the Germans in 1939 and distinguished themselves as pilots during the Battle of Britain.

One day early in 1944, the religion teacher, Father Stefanowski, called me to his room and told me that some of the older children had been asking him why I never went to communion. He had explained that I had never taken the catechism lessons necessary before first communion and then dropped a bombshell – I would have to leave the institution because he was starting a group of pre-communicants my age and the excuse that he had given to them would no longer be valid.

I asked Father Stefanowski why I couldn't join this group, learn the catechism, have my first communion and continue to keep my secret. He replied that only Christians could go to communion. Why couldn't I become a Christian? I asked. He said that I could, but I would have to learn the catechism. I told him that I was willing to do so. I gave no thought to the possible repercussions of my sudden decision – all I wanted was to find a way to stay. I was in the safest place I had experienced since being stranded outside the ghetto. In response, Father Stefanowski opened one of his large desk drawers, took out a small paperback book and told me to read it from cover to cover. When I was finished, he would "ask me my catechism" (that is, test my knowledge of it) and answer any questions I might have. He paused and then said emphatically that when I knew my catechism he would baptize me. I would then be a Christian.

For the next few weeks, I studied my catechism whenever time permitted and was rather proud to be among the very small group of older boys and girls who were to be my fellow first communicants. A few days before our first communion, Father Stefanowski again called me to his room and we went through the last lesson. He said that I mustn't feel that I was being forced into baptism, but if I became a Christian, I would be required to behave like one. This would mean attending mass and going to confession and communion. I nodded in agreement.

Father Stefanowski put on his scapular, his religious robe, and began the baptism ceremony. When it was finished, he shook my hand and said that I was now free of original sin, as pure as the driven snow. If I were to die on the spot, I would go straight to heaven. I kissed his hand and he lightened the moment with a few jokes, welcoming me into the Catholic Church. I asked him very seriously, "Father, can I become a priest?" and without hesitation, he replied, "Of course!" Then I asked, "Can I become a bishop or a cardinal?" He told me that he personally knew of a bishop of Jewish origin, but he added quickly, "We'll stop right here." He thus prevented me from asking the final question, "Can I become the Pope?" That would be going too far.

The days before my first communion were difficult for me. I thought about my family, especially my grandmother, who had been very observant. I thought about my occasional visits to the synagogue with my father. Although I hadn't understood the Hebrew prayers, I had enjoyed the singing of the *chazzan* (cantor). I remembered that converts to Christianity were not well regarded by Jews, whatever their motivation might be. I felt like a traitor to my own people, especially to my family. Yet, life had to go on and I eventually came to a conclusion that saved my sanity: I had a right to live and if conversion enabled me to survive, so be it. Although now I don't practise any religion, my conversion left its mark; to this day, I cannot tolerate ridicule of any religion.

Life with the Salesians seemed like paradise. I always had enough to eat despite my unwilling donations to the ever-hungry prefect. He and I were now in a state of truce. Although we knew each other's secret, we never discussed the matter. One day, to my surprise, the prefect told the boys at breakfast that he had been asked to nominate a second-in-command for our group, to be chosen by both the prefect and the director. The boy named was none other than Piotr Grodzieński. The younger boys accepted the news gracefully – if I was old enough to shower alone, I was surely old enough to be vice-prefect.

One day, during a recreation period supervised only by a woman teacher whose name now escapes me, I asked her a few banal questions as a lead-in to the questions that really interested me. I was thirsty for news of the outside world. Ignoring my efforts, however, she started asking me questions about my religious beliefs. My internal alarm immediately went off. She clearly sensed my unease and said that she was only trying to be a good teacher, that she was asking the questions to better understand and help us. What followed, inadequately camouflaged, was a series of questions about my confessions. How did I prepare myself? How completely did I reveal my sins to the priest? How did he behave?

No matter how hard the teacher tried to pull the wool over my eyes, I became certain that she was Jewish and that she was preparing to pass as a gentile. All the information she gathered from me and other sources would make it possible for her to go to confession without revealing that she was Jewish. We were both saved by the bell indicating the end of the recreation period. I never did find out what happened to her, since life in the institution and in Warsaw was overtaken by events of international importance that changed my life completely once more.

The Warsaw Uprising

Summer was fast approaching, and, along with it, the powerful Soviet army. Air raids were now a daily occurrence. The sirens began as soon as the German air defence detected planes over Warsaw, followed by the powerful German anti-aircraft searchlights crisscrossing the sky. Shortly after that we heard the roar of planes and saw the brightly coloured bullets of the anti-aircraft guns mingling with the beams of the searchlights; the scene was spectacular. We began a new game of gambling on the fate of each plane and on the number of hits the gunners would score, but the Soviet planes heading for Berlin flew too high.

After witnessing a few of these air raids, my excitement took the form of a constantly gurgling stomach. My emotional state was fed by rumours, predictions, speculations and some limited facts about what was going on around us. The wilder rumours included stories that the Americans were going to drop thousands of paratroopers into the middle of Warsaw; that the Soviet army was already on the other side of the Vistula River, preparing to coordinate their ground attack with the American paratrooper drop; and that the partisans were planning to come into Warsaw from the forests and seize the bridges to facilitate the Soviet troops' entry into the city. This last piece of gossip turned out to be based on an actual agreement between the Polish underground and the Soviet army.

August 1, 1944 was filled with excitement and confusion. Father Stefanowski asked me to walk to a certain address to pick up hosts for communion, and I was thrilled to be able to see for myself what was going on in the streets. I saw groups of young men and women, as well as some older adults, standing near walls that had been recently plastered with posters of different sizes. After ensuring that there were no German soldiers or Gestapo agents around, I stopped to read one that called on the Polish people to rise up, to join one of the resistance groups fighting for the liberation of Warsaw and Poland. The poster proclaimed that the "holy war" was only a few hours away. Other posters stated that the Soviet army and Polish contingents would be crossing the Vistula to join the uprising.

Highly excited and fighting tears of joy, I saw numerous young men with guns hanging from their shoulders under open jackets. Many of them wore red and white armbands embossed with the initials of a political party. They didn't have uniforms, but to me they looked like the best dressed and equipped soldiers I had ever seen. They looked at their watches every few minutes, which confirmed to me that the uprising would, as some of the posters had promised, start at 4:00 p.m. that day.

When I arrived at my destination, I checked the posters again to see how much time I had left, and I ran back through streets that were now empty of normal traffic. The usual German foot patrols were conspicuously absent. Open troop carriers raced through the streets, sirens screaming, filled with heavily armed German soldiers. Huge machine guns, with chains of bullets hanging from their loading sides, were mounted on the front and back of these trucks.

News of the uprising was already public knowledge at the institution. We were told to get ready for 4:00 p.m., now only a few hours away. As one of the oldest boys I had few friends close to my age, but we all started talking about what to do. It quickly became obvious that we each had a different plan and in the end only one other boy and I wanted to join the army. I was thrilled at the prospect of fighting for liberation and revenge, but what I couldn't discuss with anyone was that my first priority after the uprising – which I assumed would succeed – would be to find out what had happened to my family. For now, I couldn't give up my false identity.

My would-be comrade-in-arms and I agreed that we would wait for the first signs of engaged battle before telling Pan Kapusta of our plans and asking for his permission to leave. The meeting with him in the courtyard went the way we had hoped – he congratulated us on our bravery in Poland's hour of need. He suggested that we prepare everything that night and leave the following morning. For the moment, we joined the rest of the students and adult personnel outside on the street. Our ears were bombarded by the constant sound of small-arms and machine-gun fire. Some boys were sure that the small-arms fire came from underground fighters and that the heavier machine guns were still in German hands. As I scanned the street and the buildings, I was touched by the sight of many different sizes of Polish flags suspended from windows, balconies and gates, all fluttering in the breeze.

The most compelling sight on that unforgettable first day, however, was a platoon of resistance fighters coming toward us. The onlookers broke into jubilant cheers. To us, these heroes were angels come to deliver us from the depths of hell. They were without doubt a motley crew – at no time during the uprising did I see units of more than one political party marching together under one commander. The only thing they had in common was the look in their eyes, burning with the desire for revenge.

The officer in charge, realizing the importance of the moment, stopped to answer the multitude of questions from the crowd, many of which concerned the situation on specific streets, most likely where relatives lived. Questions of a military nature were perfunctorily rejected. At the end of the soldiers' rest period, our kitchen department brought out several trays of cookies and cakes, which prompted wild applause from both soldiers and civilians. When calm was finally restored and the commanding officer gave the order to march on, the crowd spontaneously burst into the Polish national anthem, with the soldiers joining in. By this time it was a beautiful summer evening, with stars twinkling overhead in a granite-blue sky.

Seeing the passing platoon had cemented my resolve to join the army the next morning. Sleep did not come easily that night but after a little while, tiredness and excitement from the day's events caught up with me and I fell into a deep sleep.

After breakfast the next morning, when my comrade and I said goodbye to everyone in the refectory, I was surprised at the reactions. Some were visibly jealous; some promised to follow in our footsteps in a day or two; and even the youngest children (nine or ten years old) asked us if the army would take them despite their age. In fact, I was soon to find out first-hand that nine- and ten-year-olds were indeed carrying out vital and dangerous functions on the front lines – running messages, which often cost them their lives. I was touched by the respect that the children and the adults showed us.

We picked up our knapsacks containing our very few belongings and a food parcel from the kitchen staff and had a brief farewell meeting with Pan Kapusta. He said that he was proud that his institution had produced such young soldiers for the uprising and for Poland. He told us about the various political groups participating in the fight, explaining that, although they were all fighting to liberate Poland, they did not see eye to eye on many other points. Without influencing us politically, his message was a clear warning about the many choices that we would be facing. Finally, he handed us our identification papers and told us to "Go with God." That was the last time I saw him.

My comrade and I went out the gate and walked to a converted storefront that served as one of many recruiting centres for the AK. I asked one of the soldiers standing there how we could volunteer and he motioned us inside, saying that it was very simple: we just had to sign up. We went in and walked up to a wide desk with several soldiers behind it, gave our names and ages, and said that we had no past or present affiliation with the German occupying forces or any communist or socialist party. The recruiter then briefed us, saying, "Citizens, you are joining the AK by registering with the Fifth Reserve Battalion, under the command of Captain Orżech, a veteran of the 1939 campaign. You must never reveal to anyone your real name and must adopt a pseudonym, here and now. You will have the right, when on guard, to challenge both civilian and military personnel by asking for the password, which will change often. Only military people, when asked for the password, have the right, after giving it, to ask you for the *réplique* [answering password]."

The interview ended with each of us signing a recruitment form that was co-signed by our interviewer since we were underage. I was given the position of adjutant to Captain Orżech. My comrade was given a similar position, but in a different unit a few streets away. He and I parted with a handshake and a military salute, although we soon learned that it was forbidden to salute anyone not wearing a military head cover. A few minutes later, a man dressed almost like a soldier came in and his bearing somehow told me that he must be an officer. I was right. Captain Orżech was probably about thirty-five, of medium height, slim and muscular. He had a pleasant face, with a high forehead and large brown eyes. I immediately felt his magnetism – this was a man I could take orders from and look up to without fear.

Captain Orżech regarded me for a moment and then described my duties as his adjutant and, more generally, as a soldier. I was expected to be at his disposal twenty-four hours a day. I was to sleep on the floor in the bedroom in his two-room quarters, which also served as his office, separated from his part of the room by a makeshift partition. I was forbidden to discuss anything I overheard while on duty. I found out later that one of my functions would be to make tours of our quarters, as often as time permitted, and verify that the soldiers' weapons, as well as all grenades, were on safety lock. As we walked among the sleeping soldiers, many of whom were holding their guns or grenades in their hands, I had to carefully pry open their fingers to remove the weapon. In many cases, the safety lock had been removed and the weapon could have discharged very easily. The safety locks were then activated and the weapons were put into a corner. Performing this duty scared me to death for a long time, although the captain was always near me.

Besides carrying orders to and from the captain, I was the link between the captain and the soldiers in our platoon. If someone wanted to change his duty shift, for example, or visit his relatives, he had to get permission through me. I immediately grew in stature with my new position; in my mind's eye, I saw myself receiving military salutes from other soldiers. The captain then told me to choose my pseudonym – I chose Gniazdo, the Polish word for nest. I knew that many soldiers chose the names of birds as their pseudonyms. Captain Orżech finished by very seriously repeating that one of the most fundamental rules of communication in the army was that a soldier, even of the lowest rank, had the right when on duty to challenge a high-ranking officer by asking for the password. The latter then had the right to demand the *réplique* from the soldier. When a soldier challenged a civilian, however, the soldier had the right to ask the civilian for the password, but the civilian didn't have the right to demand the *réplique*. This important rule was strictly observed for security reasons.

After these preliminaries, Captain Orżech congratulated me and wished me good luck. I didn't yet know what our platoon's role was in the uprising, or when we would be engaged in an actual battle. Part of me was afraid of being wounded or killed, but another part of me wanted to get a gun and use it against the Germans. As ordered, I was sitting outside the captain's office when a few soldiers approached me and we introduced ourselves using only our pseudonyms. They asked me about my past and I asked them about what to expect and what to do.

I was surprised that not every soldier had a gun; most of the new recruits didn't have one. The soldiers who had been in the underground for a while had procured weapons by disarming Germans during assaults on warehouses or by attacking trains loaded with weapons destined for the eastern front. New recruits usually got arms and ammunition from headquarters before being sent into action, or from a German prisoner. The soldiers started arguing about which kind of gun I should get given my size and the need for one that would be easy to operate. The winner was a German automatic pistol that held thirty-two rounds and could be adjusted to shoot one or more at a time, the forerunner of the now famous AK-47. One of the soldiers produced one and, after emptying it for safety's sake, lent it to me so that I could get the feel of it.

Over the next days our platoon executed its assigned task – to keep the German infantry and tanks from penetrating deeper into the position held by the Polish insurgents. We set up watch in a building close to a German position, knowing that the Germans would send a tank surrounded by foot soldiers as close as possible to our barricades. The tanks were equipped with a long turret-mounted cannon or a high-calibre machine gun. After the tank sprayed our position, the infantry attacked on foot, firing either old-fashioned Mausers or automatic pistols. Our platoon's role was to observe the German positions and report movements that indicated this kind of attack to the district command. On the basis of this information, our troops were sent to prevent the German advance.

Since the Polish army was short of anti-tank guns, we used Molotov cocktails. During my first battle, we allowed the approaching tank and infantry to roll down the street toward our barricades and penetrate our position to a certain depth, then our teenaged soldiers launched enough Molotov cocktails from both sides of the street to set the tank ablaze. This forced the soldiers inside to scramble out to escape a fiery death and the few who survived the fire were picked off by our snipers. Immediately after the attack on the tank, we ran for cover. The German infantry, which had now lost the cover of the tank, were sprayed by machine gun fire from our second group of fighters hidden on the higher floors of the buildings on both sides of the street. Most of the time, the Germans surrendered rather than face certain death. At the end of this battle I had managed to take a pistol and ammunition belt from a dead German soldier.

Although our unit was labelled "reserve" and rarely took part in a frontal attack, we were constantly called into action. After several days of fighting, the Germans barricaded themselves in the few buildings and compounds they had occupied since 1939. From a bird's eye view, you would see islands controlled by the German army almost entirely surrounded by Polish fighters. The German "islands" were of different sizes. It might comprise an entire suburb because of its geographical position or a single high-rise building in the city centre, impregnable because it was built of concrete. We didn't have enough soldiers, heavy-calibre arms or ammunition to dislodge them.

We arrived at a stalemate in less than two weeks, during which shots were exchanged and occasional attacks were launched by our side in hopes of dislodging the Germans from their strongholds. The Germans, however, were extremely well stocked with food, weapons and ammunition, as if they had taken precautions well in advance. Nevertheless, they had difficulty procuring medical supplies since we had cut them off from their supply lines. Every so often we experienced a German counterattack aimed at breaking our siege and re-establishing their supply lines. After five years of occupation, we had no sympathy for the Germans, but we obeyed the Geneva Convention, as they did, organizing half-hour truces so that each side could retrieve its dead and wounded. Meanwhile, the population of Warsaw settled down to wait, hoping for a quick conclusion.

After a few weeks of waiting for outside help, the moral and material support for the uprising began to fade. We increasingly heard criticism and blame directed at the insurgents, although everyone knew that the Soviet army stationed in Praga had promised to cross into the city at the start of the uprising. Everyone also knew that they had moved back instead of fulfilling their promise.

A few days after I enlisted, I began to feel antisemitic currents in my unit. None of the factions in the uprising was officially antisemitic and no one ever asked me directly if I was Jewish, since that would have resulted in a court-martial. Nevertheless, some of my comrades, when talking to me, adopted a nasal, singing twang that caricatured the Jewish accent in Polish. This was their way of saying that they knew I was Jewish and that they could get away with this mockery. The irony was that I had survived up to this point because I didn't have the accent they were caricaturing. My response was to tell the whole unit that I was indeed Jewish, that I was proud of it, and that I was proud to do my part to liberate Poland. My status as Captain Orżech's adjutant allowed me certain privileges, which may have provoked the antisemitism. One day, a visiting chaplain who knew I was Jewish told me that he had learned there was a conspiracy in my unit to get rid of me. When Captain Orżech got wind of this, he ordered a roll call and without mincing words, informed the men that he would punish anyone who lifted a finger against me. This was the first and last time that my being Jewish led to this kind of confrontation while I was in the army.

Our unit was also used to enforce law and order among the civilian population. Since the Germans often cut the water in certain areas, civilians had to stand in long lines at the few wells that had been dug in 1939 between battles. As might be expected, the people waiting in line were tired, hungry and impatient, and were losing hope in the uprising, prompting physical fights over everything and nothing. At that point we had to intervene. One day, after we restored peace to one of these lines, a civilian thanked us on behalf of the others, as if he were in charge of the line. Feeling very important, I stupidly retorted, in my almost non-existent German, "Ordnung muß sein!" (There must be order!) Pandemonium broke loose, with many in the crowd crying, "Let's hang this German!" The officer in charge of our unit was able to diffuse the collective fury by ordering me to disappear, which I did.

When I recounted this incident to one of my comrades, he laughed uncontrollably, calling me the most insulting names that Polish had to offer. Listening to this litany, I absentmindedly put my hand into a metal pail that contained sand to fight fires. Letting the sand seep through my fingers had a soothing effect, and each time I immersed my hand, it went deeper and deeper into the bucket. Eventually my hand touched a metal object and my fingers closed around it. When I pulled my hand out of the sand, I saw to my horror that I was holding an English or American hand grenade with a corrugated surface designed to increase its cluster-bomb effect.

My friend ordered me not to move, not to release the pressure of my fingers on the grenade. He put his hand over my hand holding the grenade and yelled for help. A few men came out of headquarters with guns at the ready. One of them was luckily an expert in explosives, who explained that these grenades had double safety locks. The second lock couldn't be opened unless the first had been sharply and strongly removed. In our case, since I hadn't dislodged the first lock, the grenade couldn't explode. Nevertheless, he congratulated us, especially my comrade, for resisting the urge to panic and calling for help.

Two close calls in one day were enough for me. I realized that the uprising was not like the game of cowboys and Indians I played with Józek before the war. This was a very real battle, in which people were being killed and wounded. Little did I know that the uprising had now run half its course. Both the left and the right factions of the Polish army had had to accept the fact that the Soviet army had retreated instead of crossing the Vistula. Consequently, our efforts to hold the bridges intact, so costly in human lives, had been worse than useless, for they had helped the German defence.

The Soviets had made a few air drops, but they were badly coordinated and the arms were quite often dropped close to the German positions. Drops that had been promised by the Polish government in London had never come to anything – there was only one huge drop executed by the American air force in mid-September. Furthermore, the drop was made from such a great height that most of it fell wide of the target and right into German hands.

The morning after the drop, the Germans paid us back with interest. They began to shell the centre of Warsaw, which by now was the only source of effective opposition. The daily military reports revealed a small but steady loss of neighbourhoods to the Germans, which forced both the army and civilians into the centre of town. The sewers were both the best and the worst conduit for this flight. I saw thousands of people emerging from the sewers with only the belongings they could carry. I heard stories about people drowning or dying of exhaustion, wounds and heart attacks in the sewers, and being left there by desperate relatives. We came to believe, during this second month of the uprising, that while the Allies were biding their time or fighting on other fronts, we were being left to bleed to death in our effort to liberate Poland.

That afternoon, during a lull in the German bombardment, a group of fighters abandoned their position in the Stare Miasto neighbourhood and they, too, retreated to the centre of Warsaw through the sewers. There were about sixty men and women followed by countless civilians who preferred fleeing toward the unknown to being taken prisoner by the Germans. The day was sunny and quiet and despite the burned-out houses, dead animals and terrible stench, people seemed relaxed, as if reconciled to this terrible reality. I saw a military unit emerge from the sewer and move toward the partially burned concert hall on Jasna Street that had been turned into one of the barracks of the insurgency. At the front of the column marched its commanding officer, looking tired but not defeated as they marched into the hall.

Suddenly, I heard a missile that we called the "cow" because it sounded like the moo of that animal as it fell, followed by a horrific explosion. I yelled, "The concert hall!" and started to run toward the building, which was now burning and badly damaged. For several hours, no one could get into the hall because of the heat generated by the powerful explosion, heat so intense that it melted the iron in the building's structure. About a thousand people participated in the attempted rescue, yet it was all in vain; we eventually retrieved fifty-nine corpses. The unit commander had survived but had apparently lost his mind. This was the largest slaughter I had witnessed during the uprising.

A group of German prisoners was brought in from a nearby detention centre to cart out the victims of the explosion. The surviving unit commander picked up a stone when he saw the German prisoners and with lightning speed crushed the head of one the Germans. A few days later, I heard that the commander was declared insane.

During the uprising, the British Broadcasting Corporation (BBC) had been broadcasting excerpts from a famous Polish poem written during one of the many battles for Poland in recent centuries, called "Ogniem i mieczem" (With Fire and Sword). I remember being furious at the British and all the other allies – while we had been risking our lives, they did nothing for us except broadcast poetry, as though we needed this inspiration to continue fighting. We needed arms and ammunition, not poetry from centuries ago. Hearing the poem only made us feel more helpless, frustrated and bitter.

On the way back to our barracks that day, we came upon a group of civilians who were burying people killed in a recent raid. Some of the bodies were grotesquely disfigured; most of them had their mouths open with what looked like intestines protruding from them, the result of a certain type of bomb that caused choking. The mass grave was a crater created by a bomb. One of the gravediggers jumped into the grave and, standing on the last corpse in the row, pulled the dead man's hand from under him, staring at a ring on the cadaver's finger. After a few unsuccessful attempts to slide the ring off, the gravedigger pulled a folding knife out of his pocket and sliced off the man's finger with the ring on it. I vomited. With my head down near the sidewalk and my whole body trembling, I heard screaming and shouting. Then, a single shot, followed by silence. Turning toward this sound, I saw one of my comrades putting his gun back into its holster. The gravedigger was lying on top of his victim.

As the territory held by the fighters shrank, the movement of ci-vilians increased as they tried to avoid capture by the Germans. Units like ours were ordered to stand guard at barricades to verify each civilian's identity before letting him enter the section of town we were guarding. We also gave information about the places people were trying to get to because many no longer existed. The information was extremely important since the Germans had snipers hidden in abandoned buildings. A German sniper hiding in an attic in a corner building had a perfect view of two streets and could pick off civilians or soldiers at random, terrifying the whole population and creating havoc. The movement of civilians usually took place at night, which offered some protection. On the other hand, snipers lurked in the attics at night, too.

One of my comrades and I were ordered to the top floor of a ma-jor downtown building. Our sentry positions were in an overpass above the street, standing back to back, twenty or thirty feet apart, each of us looking out a window. Together, we had a perfect view of anyone trying to cross the street from any point. There were two high-powered rifles mounted on the window sill and the sentry with the longer view had a built-in telescope on his rifle. We had to be ready to shoot at any moment and this nerve-wracking sentry duty lasted about an hour and a half.

I was very excited, for this was the first time that I had been as-signed this exacting task. I had been chosen because of my excellent results during target practice and had been promoted to the status of sharpshooter. I took my position and began to acquaint myself with the impressive rifle that I would be in charge of for the next ninety minutes. The territory that I was to survey was one city block and consisted of a street lined with buildings, with stores on the ground floor and apartments above.

After a few minutes of silence, my comrade and I started to talk as a way to keep alert and fight boredom since the streets were deserted. Time passed – perhaps half an hour. Then my comrade asked me to replace him because he needed to answer nature's call and wanted a smoke. Since his survey territory was longer than mine, he wanted me to take his position on the grounds that it was more vital and the previous guard had said that his side was more active. Our orders forbade us to leave our posts to smoke or even to hold conversations, so I refused. After a few more minutes of silence, I asked my fellow sentry a question. Getting no reply, I repeated it in a louder voice. When even that got no reaction, I turned around, and found my comrade slumped over the window sill with a bullet hole through his forehead.

We had not been told what to do in this situation. I couldn't establish if the man was alive or dead. Even if he were alive, I had no first-aid equipment or training, nor did I have any way of getting in touch with headquarters. I tried to control my panic. I decided to leave my post and go to headquarters, although it was forbidden to abandon a position without authorization. On the way, I prepared my defence – I had not been told what to do in this kind of emergency. At headquarters, I made my report and, strangely enough, was not reprimanded. The body of my unfortunate comrade was retrieved and buried in a freshly dug grave, and after a short prayer and homily by our chaplain, we dispersed. I realized again how dangerous our work really was and how insignificant all our little troubles were next to the closeness of death.

A few days later, I was assigned night sentry duty with another soldier. Our shift was to last four hours and was not considered to be dangerous because we expected mostly civilians to pass through our lines. As we prepared to go to our sentry position from midnight to 4:00 a.m., my comrade checked our weapons. We both had automatic pistols and my partner also carried a homemade lantern. Before we started out, he looked at me shyly but hopefully and asked if I would mind if his girlfriend visited him at the barricade. We both knew, of course, that this was forbidden. Nevertheless, I was fourteen years old and this request activated not only my imagination but also my hormones. Without hesitation, I agreed to go along with this secret tryst, although I stopped short of asking him to ask his girlfriend to bring along a girl for me.

The barricade was composed of cement blocks and furniture of all kinds, even mattresses. At one end there was an opening through which people could pass; at the other was a small opening to an en-closure, something like a shack. Shortly after we relieved the previ-ous guards, a young woman appeared and, after introducing her, my comrade took her by the hand and headed for the shack. Just before they reached it, he turned and winked at me.

Alone, my vivid imagination was occupied by what was happening in the shack. The night progressed, the movement of civilians dimin-ished and I started to get bored, debating with myself as to whether it was time to interrupt the tryst. Suddenly, I heard rhythmic steps that sounded like military marching. I swung my automatic pistol across my chest and adopted the "at ready" position. A moment later, a man carrying a large suitcase passed through the gate, put the suitcase down and looked around. He hadn't noticed me so I stepped forward and shouted for him to stop, even though he had already done so. I asked him what was in his suitcase and the purpose of his trip, for it was unusual for civilians to travel alone. His answers were plausible and to this day, I don't know what made me ask him for the password. Most civilians didn't know the password, which changed frequently, so it would have been normal for the man to profess ignorance of it. But he not only gave me the correct password, which, as a civilian, was the maximum that he should have known, he also asked me for the *réplique*, which was forbidden to civilians. This was his undoing.

Pointing my pistol at him, I shouted, "Hands up and turn toward the wall!" To my great relief, I heard my comrade running toward us. Covering the suspicious traveller with his gun, he told me to open the suitcase. There was nothing out of the ordinary about the carefully cleaned, pressed and folded clothes. We were mainly looking for weapons, but also photos that could provide clues as to whether he was a Polish-speaking German or a *Volksdeutsch* – the Germans loved photography and a picture could be evidence of this identity. Unable to find anything suspicious, I started to replace the contents of the suitcase. My comrade told me to cover the man and grabbed the suitcase, turned it upside down and began to examine it very carefully. His efforts were rewarded – it had a double bottom. He opened the secret compartment and we found several papers that identified the man as a *Volksdeutsch*. The *pièce à conviction* (incriminating evidence), however, was a flogging apparatus, a short-handled leather cat-o'-nine-tails with tiny lead balls at the end of each cord.

The man begged us to let him explain, his tearful voice betraying his fear. Since my comrade was in command, he ordered me to go to our quarters and bring help, and to escort his girlfriend to her home near our barracks on the way. At our quarters I explained to the night guard what had happened and he woke up three men to accompany me to the barricade. They took the prisoner to AK headquarters, at which point our responsibility ended. I never learned his fate.

By this time it was morning and during roll call, Captain Orżech commended my comrade and me for being alert and performing our duty, even though it had seemed like an ordinary night watch. After being dismissed, my comrade shook my hand and again gave me a wink, which I returned this time with feigned nonchalance.

Next, our unit was ordered to replace another one that had just suffered the loss of three soldiers who had been on guard duty in an unfamiliar building. We deduced that they must have been captured because we hadn't heard any shots during the night. We looked around for safe places to post our guards and installed primitive alarm systems such as a cord attached to a bottle. If a guard was about to be captured he could pull the cord so the bottle would fall and break with a crash. Containers filled with stones on window sills worked similarly. The problem that we couldn't solve was our hunger since we were not equipped for operations that lasted many hours. We began to look around for food, but these had been office buildings and, although we found all sorts of things, there was not a morsel in sight.

As I looked from store to store on the ground floor, the situation reminded me of the time in the ghetto when Stach and I found food in an apartment but almost paid for this discovery with our lives. I became very depressed and for a long moment couldn't think of anything but my lost family.

I was woken from my trance by a command to stop, followed by the commanding officer's order to assemble. He said that searching any farther away from the rest of our unit would be dangerous and ordered us back to our original position. When we got there, the men had made a few fires in the courtyard and were boiling water for tea. A civilian at one of the fires was talking amiably to the soldiers. Our commanding officer asked the man who he was and if he could find us some food. He replied that he was the janitor of these three buildings, but his own apartment was in German-held territory. Suddenly, he jumped up and, striking his forehead, started to laugh hysterically, repeating how stupid he was. When he calmed down, he said that if he could take two men with him for half an hour, he would treat us to a feast. There was a shack on the ground floor of a neighbouring building and in it was a goat that had belonged to one of the tenants. If the goat had not escaped or been taken away, we would have a fine supper. Our commandant chose two soldiers for the detail, who happily grabbed their guns and disappeared with the janitor.

Our goat hunters returned carrying a large dead animal on a pike, its body so badly burned that some of us, including me, refused to eat it. A few volunteers, however, took the dead animal to a corner of the courtyard and began to clean and cut up the carcass. Just as we were settling down for the night, there was a shriek from the soldiers who were eating the "goat" and several of them were vomiting. One of them pointed to a shiny object on the neck of the animal. It was the metal tag on a dog collar. The janitor told us shakily that animals other than the goat must have been kept in the shack. When they had arrived at the burnt-out shack, they had taken the first carcass they saw. Our commander told the janitor to leave immediately. Although this demoralizing incident had not been his fault, his safety could no longer be guaranteed.

The next day, a large unit of fighters joined us at our position and we all fanned out looking for Germans and our three missing comrades. After a day of searching we came upon an abandoned German position containing many of their supplies. They had apparently had an escape route and retreated from their position rather than try to break our lines. Our operation was concluded and our comrades were never found. Tired and discouraged, we returned to our base.

Surrender and Flight

During the next few days, there was almost no fighting. The civilian population came up out of the shelters and mingled restlessly in the streets. It was the end of September and there were rumours that the military high command was negotiating a truce with the German army. It felt like the beginning of the end, a feeling that was soon vindicated when we learned that the Germans had accepted our surrender.

An officer addressed us from a makeshift podium, ordering us to attention for three minutes in solidarity with our fallen comrades. He tried to explain our defeat by referring to the failures of our allies, without ever naming them. He assured us that the capitulation agreement was between the Polish army and the Wehrmacht; the SS and other contingents notorious for their cruelty had not been present at the signing. The officer concluded by saying that despite this defeat, the proverbial light at the end of the tunnel was much closer than before the uprising.

Just before distributing our pay, which in my case was the equivalent of ten American dollars, the speaker told us that we must be prepared for the separation of officers from private soldiers. Another officer explained how the march to the prisoner of war camp in Pruszków would be organized: we were to leave Warsaw with our arms and ammunition and deposit them at the feet of the first Wehrmacht contingent that we encountered.

At the end of the speech, we picked up our weapons and started toward Pruszków. Just before reaching the highway, we arrived at a German outpost, where each of us placed his weapon on the ground at the feet of a German soldier, then continued marching stoically. I must admit that the worst predictions for this stage of the surrender turned out to be wrong – some of us believed that the Wehrmacht guards would be replaced by the hated SS and Ukrainian soldiers. The march continued uneventfully, however, and our unit of about fifty men was guarded by only six German soldiers, two at the head, one on each side and two in the rear. They were only lightly armed older men who didn't seem very fierce to us.

About half an hour after having given up our weapons, we were ordered to stop marching and rest. Captain Orżech took me aside where no one could hear us. Without mincing words, he told me that even though I was his adjutant, he could not protect me since I was not an officer and would not be imprisoned with him. As a Jew, I would be discovered at the first medical exam. To make matters worse, some of our men might betray me for a small reward from the Germans.

Satisfied that I understood the gravity of my situation, Captain Orżech told me that he had a plan for my escape. At the approach of dusk, near a drainage ditch, he and a few trustworthy members of our unit would create a diversion to draw the guards to the front of the column. The ditches, located at roughly quarter-kilometre intervals, contained enormous cement pipes that were big enough for a person to stand in. The captain would place me at the end of the column so I could run down into the drainage pipe during the diversion. I was to wait there until nightfall and then go to the nearest village and ask for directions to Łowicz, about eighty kilometres away. Captain Orżech gave me the name of a truck driver, Kazimierczak, who was an active AK member working for the Germans there. He assured me that by mentioning his pseudonym, I would get the help I needed in Łowicz. With the traditional Polish "May God be with you!" the captain re-

sumed his position. At dusk, as we arrived at a drainage ditch and
pipe, a fight broke out as promised. All the German guards rushed to
the head of the column to break it up and I quickly slid into the ditch
and ran into the pipe. I still wonder to this day if Captain Orżech was
Jewish or if I reminded him of a loved one. Why did he take such care
to help me at the beginning of our relationship and, at the end, take
such a risk to save my life?

I found two other people in the drainage pipe, a young woman
and a boy of my age, who had escaped from a similar column made
up entirely of civilians from Warsaw. When the last columns of civilians and soldiers had passed, we left the shelter of the drainage
pipe and headed toward the nearest small town, just visible on the
horizon. The town was full of people, both civilians and military, who
had also managed to escape from the march to Pruszków. Some of
the residents gave us shelter when we promised to leave the following
morning.

In the morning, a constant stream of vehicles whizzed by toward
the west, in the direction of Łowicz and, farther on, Lodz. They were
not only the usual military vehicles, but also private cars filled with
German civilians who, like the Poles, were evacuating Warsaw before the Soviet onslaught. Seeing German civilians running for their
lives was a sight for sore eyes. A high-ranking German officer in an
open car stopped in front of our little group and asked our young
woman companion if he could take her to Lodz. She turned to the
other young boy and me as if she needed our permission, then got
into the car without a word. Then the boy shook my hand, turned
away and disappeared. I was left alone with no idea of how to get to
Łowicz until a woman old enough to be my mother appeared out of
nowhere and said that she had heard me asking the way to Łowicz.
She in fact lived there and was about to start out for home on foot,
hoping to hitch a ride on a farmer's wagon. Our journey together
lasted more than a day, during which we each cautiously tried to find
out about each other.

Eventually, the woman told me her story. She and her family, her husband and her teenage daughter, came from Łowicz. Her daughter had been caught by the Germans and sent to Germany as slave labour. Her husband was working in Łowicz and the two of them, for practical reasons, had moved in with her parents. She happened to have been in Warsaw at the beginning of the uprising and this was the first time that she had been able to return home. Hearing that her parents had always lived in Łowicz and that her husband was working there, I asked if she knew a man named Kazimierczak.

When she heard his name, the woman crossed herself and asked me why I had mentioned him. I told her my well-rehearsed story, that my parents had been killed by the Germans, that I had then lived in an orphanage and had joined the uprising, but now was trying to avoid being sent to Germany because of my age and delicate health. The name Kazimierczak had been given to me by a fellow soldier. Looking surprised, she told me that Kazimierczak was her husband. Tears of astonishment and relief stung my eyes. I told her that the soldier who had given me her husband's name had also told me of his double life. As we approached Łowicz, she told me that although her parents were very old and the house would not normally accommodate five people, she would let me stay there until the end of the war, which everyone knew was at hand.

The house was a duplex with two apartments side by side. A couple who had escaped from Bydgoszcz lived in the half not occupied by the woman's family. The man, Piotr Konikowski, had been the town's railroad stationmaster. I came to like and respect him, and visited him in his hometown after the war. When we arrived at the house, I was introduced to the elderly parents of Mrs. Kazimierczak and, a little later, to the Konikowski couple. Mr. Konikowski was in his mid-thirties, short, soft-spoken, and an entertaining talker. His wife was a slim woman, more than a head taller than her husband. Seeing a grown man who was shorter than I, married, who held a responsible job, was well read and clearly gifted gave me hope for myself. Later the same evening, Mr. Kazimierczak came home from his job as a truck driver for the German army. In contrast to Mr. Konikowski, Pan Kazimierczak was over six feet tall, bald and around two hundred pounds. He was a powerful bundle of energy and I was glad not to have him as an enemy. Unlike Konikowski, he was uncomplicated, deeply religious and taciturn.

During the next few days, I spent much of my time with Mr. Konikowski, who always had something interesting to say. Mrs. Kazimierczak and her mother were good cooks. The food was simple but sufficient, which was a welcome change from my experiences in Warsaw. At the outset, nights presented a problem because there wasn't enough room or beds for five people. Mr. Kazimierczak solved the problem by putting two chairs together for me to sleep on. He put old coats and blankets on top and, given my youth, I slept well.

A few days later, Mrs. Kazimierczak's parents complained about me to their daughter. The atmosphere became tense, I got nervous and my alarm bells started ringing. I think that the old couple may have suspected that I was Jewish and were afraid that a neighbour would come to the same conclusion and turn the family into the Germans. Mrs. Kazimierczak took me aside and told me that it was not a good idea for me to stay at the house, which after all, belonged to her parents. She asked if I would mind working as an apprentice at a tailor shop in Łowicz run by lay brothers. She was sure that the brothers would take me in since she knew the head brother, Żak, personally. I agreed right away and Mrs. Kazimierczak and I walked into town.

Mr. Żak was a pleasant-looking man with a ruddy complexion that was probably due to his love of alcohol, something he made no effort to hide. Unlike some of my previous shelters, this one required no interviews or paperwork. I was simply left there by Mrs. Kazimierczak, who told me that I would be living at the shop six days a week, receiving room and board there. On Saturday nights and Sundays, I would be welcome at her house.

The tailor shop had three full-time tailors and three apprentices, including me. All except one full-time worker and me lived in Łowicz and went home at night. Meals were served downstairs in a dining hall where we were joined by other lay brothers, making about twenty people in all. The other live-in worker and I slept in two huge chests, with plenty of material, blankets, and old coats to keep us warm and comfortable. This new place felt safe to me, far away from the Germans. There was no great danger of my being discovered as a Jew and I was eager to learn how to become a good tailor.

One day, Mr. Żak was serving a couple in the front room when he called me to come in and light a fire in a huge fireplace, beside which were stacked piles of dried wood. I panicked – I had never lit a fire. I began to clean out the fireplace from the previous fire and heard the customers comment on my awkwardness and lack of ability. I distinctly heard them say – only half-jokingly – that I had two left hands, and that I worked like a Jew. Mr. Żak came to my rescue by ordering me back into the workshop and asking another apprentice to make the fire. He turned this incident into a joke, remarking that people from Warsaw produced little aristocrats who were unable to even feed themselves. The fire was lit within a few minutes and the incident was never brought up again. Nevertheless, it reminded me of the danger that lurked in every corner and led me to pay close attention to what everyone – including me – said.

Mr. Żak's tailor shop, like other businesses in Łowicz, became a prime target of the newly formed social organizations that were trying to place refugees. One day Mr. Żak introduced us to a man named Smoczek who was a master tailor from Warsaw. Mr. Smoczek's wife and young daughter were living in Łowicz as well. As he became surer of himself, Mr. Smoczek began to sing while he worked. The men in the shop liked these performances and the more he sang, the more the other workers asked him to sing.

From the beginning, I suspected that Mr. Smoczek was Jewish. He was short and dark-haired, with dark brown eyes and Jewish features, and Smoczek was a Jewish-sounding name. His impeccable Polish did not have the class accent that one would expect in a tailor. One day, after the workers had asked him to sing, Mr. Smoczek announced that he was going to sing an aria from a famous opera. When he started to sing, I was electrified – it was no aria that he was singing but Kol Nidre, the prayer chanted at the beginning of Yom Kippur. As Mr. Smoczek must have intended, our eyes met and we both knew that the other was Jewish.

By the time that Christmas was approaching my life followed a routine – I worked and lived at the factory six days a week and spent my Saturday evenings and Sundays at the Kazimierczaks', which I called home. My duties at the tailor shop included cleaning the factory, lighting the fire and preparing material for the tailors. This last set of tasks included ironing moist cloth from which Mr. Żak, using a pattern, cut the garment ordered, usually a cassock. Once cut, the garment passed through different stages in our shop until it became the finished product. The European cassock had buttons down the front so finishing it involved manually making buttonholes and sewing on the buttons. That job was given to Mr. Smoczek, for no one else could do it as quickly and accurately. He posed one condition, however – that somebody else thread the needle while he sewed on each button. No matter how I tried, I could never be a few needles ahead of Smoczek; he could sew a button faster than I could thread a needle. Nevertheless, I was proud of my role in the tailoring process every time I saw a priest, regardless of whether I had worked on his cassock.

Conversations in our shop had turned to the usual predictions, rumours and half-truths about the expected arrival of the Soviet army. Although we didn't know when it would happen, we all agreed that the Germans were leaving town as fast as they could by every means of travel.

Close to Christmas, Mr. Kazimierczak asked me to accompany a nun from a small village to Łowicz. A horse and wagon had already been arranged, but the times were so dangerous, it would be better if another person was on the journey. Although I could hardly physically protect the nun, I was better than nothing. He asked me to go on foot alone from Łowicz, and after getting the directions and some clothes to protect me against the bitterly cold winter night, I set out. The winter landscape was beautiful; the dark blue sky was cloudless and sprinkled with millions of sparkling stars. New-fallen snow crackled under my feet. Every needle of the evergreen trees was covered with its own layer of snow, almost as if it had been applied individually by hand.

When I got to a bridge that I had to cross, I saw to my horror a German sentry standing at the end near me with a light machine gun in his hands. He must have been as surprised to see me as I was to see him. I knew that if I ran away, he would kill me, so I started walking toward him. In a minute, I found myself looking into the eyes of a tall, bundled-up soldier. Suddenly, he swung his gun onto his back, put his hand on my shoulder and started singing "O Tannenbaum" (O Christmas Tree). I recognized the Christmas carol because it had been piped into the square in Łowicz since the start of the Christmas season. I joined in as best I could. I don't remember how long the duet lasted, but I took the first opportunity to leave. Saying goodbye with the few German words that came to me, I started off again on my journey.

In the village I enjoyed a much-needed bowl of hot soup and my host introduced me to a woman dressed in civilian clothes who was addressed as "Sister." I was told again that my job was to take the nun to Łowicz in a horse-drawn cart and to keep my questions to myself. I felt butterflies in my stomach. Early the next morning, I was surprised to see that the nun had hidden her beautiful long black hair in the same type of wing-like headdress that I had seen on nursing nuns. After a breakfast of a hot soup-like liquid, we prepared the cart for our trip. The nun sat behind me and covered herself with the hay that had been provided by our host to keep her warm. He gave me an old goat skin that kept me very warm. Just before our departure, the nun led us in a prayer and we set off.

On the way to Łowicz, I tried to understand the purpose of this trip. I concluded that the nun must be a messenger travelling from one group of partisans to another. Being a nun transported by a young boy, she was less likely to attract suspicion. I'm still not sure if she really was a nun or a female partisan in disguise. The journey to Łowicz took several hours, but was uneventful. I left the nun, the horse and the cart at the address that I had been given and returned to the Kazimierczaks' house.

Along with the holiday music, the German propaganda machine broadcast military reports about the inevitable, relentless approach of the Soviet army. We saw panic on the faces of the Germans as they sped westward through the town. Although the Germans knew that it was now five minutes to midnight for them, they relentlessly pursued the policy of the "Final Solution." On Christmas Eve, they built a gallows for two people in the town square and just before dark brought the prisoners out in an open truck with their hands bound behind them and ropes around their necks.

In front of a small crowd, a German officer made a speech in which the word *Jude* figured prominently. When he finished, he took his place in the passenger's seat of the truck and gave the order for it to move. As the truck moved forward, the ropes, which had been attached at one end to the gallows, pulled the two men out of the truck and caused them to drop several feet to the ground, breaking their necks. The bodies remained in the square, dangling from the gallows, until the next morning, when town workers cut them down and buried them.

The new year began and on January 15, 1945, a few Soviet planes flying at a low altitude dropped several bombs on the square, which started fires but otherwise caused little damage and no deaths. It was enough, however, for Mr. Żak. He closed the shop and told us to take a short vacation. I went to the Kazimierczaks' house, where

Mr. Kazimierczak was also at home because his job no longer existed – his German employers had fled west. In the next few days, Mr. Konikowski dismantled his 120-base accordion, wrapping its components in homemade wax paper and then burying it in a well-insulated hole in the ground.

After supper on the evening of January 19, Mr. and Mrs. Konikowski came to our apartment with a large bottle of champagne. They had kept it for a very special occasion and felt that tonight was it. It was a bitterly cold but bright night, and every so often we could see through the frosty window the German soldiers escaping westward. Mr. Konikowski concluded that the Soviet army must be closing in on them.

Suddenly, we heard a military truck roll into the courtyard at the back of the house and the front door pushed open. Sixteen (I counted them!) young Wehrmacht soldiers armed with machine guns walked in and addressed us first in German and then in broken Polish. The spokesman for the group assured us that they were not volunteers, but conscripts who had been forced into the German army. They were nervous, yet they made us understand that they had been ordered to defend to the bitter end the little bridge about fifteen metres from the house. The group spokesman, now speaking only Polish and invoking the name of God repeatedly, begged us for civilian clothes and directions to the west. Another soldier collected all the guns and ammunition and put them in front of us. He insisted that they no longer wanted to fight; they only wanted to escape from the Soviets.

We gathered all the men's clothes that we could find and gave them directions from the highway. Some of them wanted to escape on foot since their truck would soon be useless for lack of gas, or worse, a target for Soviet Katyusha rockets. We took them outside and showed them a shortcut through the forest that would eventually take them to the highway where they might be picked up by a German vehicle. The Germans then broke into groups and disappeared into the night. We went back into the house to assess our odd situation. What could we do, in a matter of minutes, with all the weapons? We put the guns behind the wall facing the back garden with two of the coats that the Germans had left on top. We planned to explain to the Soviets how we had come by these German military clothes, guns and ammunition.

It was almost 11:00 p.m. when Mr. Konikowski reappeared with his bottle of champagne and gave us each a little. He took command of our group and put forward his strategy for our survival. We were afraid that the Soviets might blow up the house as they passed, so we had to hide in the potato cellar and wait to see what happened. Taking anything that we could to keep warm, including a couple of duvets and pillows, the seven of us disappeared into the potato cellar and shut the door from the inside.

Towards morning, I was awakened by Kazimierczak shaking me. Konikowski said that it was already 6:00 a.m. and despite the insulation in the potato cellar, they heard noises coming from the highway. We had to find out what the noises meant and I was chosen for the mission not because I was the smallest – Konikowski was smaller – but because I was the youngest. We hoped that whoever was outside, whether Soviets or Germans, would be less likely to kill me than an adult.

I wasn't exactly a keen volunteer and had to be gently shoved outside with words of encouragement. The morning was still grey and bitterly cold, with huge snowflakes falling on the frozen ground. I heard an unfamiliar, repetitive sound and at the same time a human voice, but I couldn't distinguish the words. As I got closer to the house, I saw a Soviet soldier coming toward me – I recognized the uniform from pictures of prisoners taken by the Germans and published in their magazines. I only knew the few Russian words I had learned from my parents when they came back from their expedition to Soviet-held territory at the start of the war. I raised my hands above my head and started yelling in Russian, "I am a Jew!" The irony of this admission did not escape me, for I had just spent two years trying desperately to sound, look and behave anything but Jewish.

The Soviet soldier turned out to be a woman who was in charge of one of the attacking tanks. She was stocky, with a machine gun across her ample chest. I didn't understand what she was saying but she put her arms around me and kissed me on both cheeks. This is how I came to be liberated. For me, the war was over and I was free.

Occupation Again

I returned to my friends in the potato cellar and told them that the highway was swarming with Soviet soldiers advancing at full speed. Within a few minutes, we went back to the house and, as the first order of business, started planning the safest way to dispose of the German weapons without being accused of collaboration. Our problem was solved when a Soviet officer entered the house demanding the use of our table, on which he placed maps and a field telephone. Kazimierczak's father-in-law took the bull by the horns and, in fluent Russian, told the officer what had happened a few hours earlier. To our surprise, the officer assured us in acceptable Polish that the Soviet army was not at war with civilians and was accustomed to finding arms and ammunition abandoned by the Germans. He opened the door and shouted an order to his troops. Several Soviet soldiers came into the house and took all the guns and ammunition away.

Mr. Konikowski and I went outside to watch the incredible scene that was unfolding. The first thing we saw was the body of a German soldier hanging from a tree. A wooden sign was attached to his genitals with an arrow pointing westward and in black letters the message in Russian, "To Berlin!"

For the first few days, the Soviet military was in charge of keeping law and order among the civilian population. Then the scene changed and Polish civil servants appeared in the town. A new Polish currency was established, a few public offices were opened and, despite the continuous movement of the mighty Soviet army toward Germany, life began to take on some normalcy.

I went back to the tailor shop and resumed as normal a life as the situation permitted. I was able to spend more time on the streets and, with the days getting longer, felt more secure. I met a few boys my age and we spent our free time among the Soviet soldiers. Within a few weeks, our tailor shop was visited by some of the higher-ranking Soviet officers, who were to remain in Łowicz for an indefinite period. They had become conscious of the poor quality and shabbiness of their uniforms. The officers brought us new material from their own supply and offered to pay for the new uniforms with fresh meat. On the day we finished the first uniform, the officer who had promised us meat showed up followed by two soldiers carrying half a calf. At the sight of the poor animal impaled on a wooden pole, dead but not skinned and dripping with blood, a few of my co-workers vomited on the spot. The Soviets burst out laughing. Mr. Żak rushed into the room, the ruler in his hand his only weapon to impose law and order. After a lengthy negotiation, in which both sides used their very limited vocabulary in the other's language, it was agreed that the Soviets would skin and prepare the calf, and bring us only the raw meat.

While spring came into full blossom, the people of Łowicz quickly learned how to coexist with the "friendly" Soviet army. There were no serious incidents although daily stories circulated about abuses by the Soviets under the pretext of military necessity. They redirected civilian traffic from major highways, for example, and reserved the use of the railway almost exclusively for their army.

After a few weeks, the routine I had settled into began to depress me and I became withdrawn and unfriendly. Soon after liberation, people in the town who had been expelled from Warsaw after the up-rising began to return to the city. I had nowhere to go, but something inside told me I should join those heading for Warsaw. Although I had only seen the partial destruction of the ghetto, I had heard enough stories to realize the futility of searching for my family there. Nevertheless, deep in my heart I knew that sooner or later, I would have to search for them.

On May 8, 1945, the public loudspeakers first installed by the Germans and then used by the Soviets broadcast the end of the war in Polish and Russian. The effect on me was miraculous. Something inside me clicked. I knew that I had to settle the question of whether any member of my family had survived, and to do this, I had to return to Warsaw. After many handshakes, pats on the shoulder, promises that I would come back to visit and wishes of "God be with you!" and "God bless you!" I found myself standing on an open freight car loaded with equipment and people heading for Warsaw. Everything that I owned was in my knapsack: one shirt, one pair of underwear, one pair of socks and a bundle of identification documents. The war had taught me that these papers would be as necessary now as they were during the German occupation.

~

When the train rolled into the main Warsaw station about an hour later, I stood in the station for a while not knowing where to go or what to do. Moving crowds of people gradually pushed me away from the station. In my mind I was picturing the streets and buildings and the train that used to take me to summer camp.

I didn't know the district I was in very well and had no idea how to get from there to the site of the ghetto. I didn't want to ask anybody where the Jewish ghetto was because such a question would identify me as a Jew, which I absolutely wanted to avoid. I suddenly recalled hiding in Dr. Płocker's apartment on Leszno Street, which was on one side of the ghetto. I asked a passing policeman for directions to Leszno Street and watched his eyes for any reaction, but I saw none. About half an hour later, I stood in front of 25 Leszno, which had not been destroyed, and was indeed Dr. Płocker's apartment. With my back to it, I faced the only Protestant church in Warsaw, which had served as a warehouse during the occupation, and which my family and I had seen while hiding in the apartment. On my left, stretching for two blocks, was the courthouse. I began to shake violently and burst into tears. The church and the courthouse were the only structures left standing. Everything else had been obliterated. Looking around me, I saw nothing but piles of bricks, stones and concrete.

After two years of anxiety, guilt and short-lived waves of hope, I was confronted with the truth. My family was gone. I was alive but alone in the world, and had to do something to survive. I congratulated myself for having outwitted the Germans and the other antisemites whose paths I had crossed during the occupation, but I knew I had to continue to hide my identity – it was not yet possible to end my double life. I only saw a future for myself as Piotr Grodzieński.

As I walked among the ruins, hoping to find something familiar, I passed two priests in cassocks and an idea came rushing into my mind – to find the Salesian-run orphanage where I had been safely hidden before. I approached the priests, kissed the hand of one of them, then told them that I was an orphan and would like to find the main office of the Salesian order. When I added that I had been living in their Warsaw orphanage until the uprising, one of the priests gave me the address of the main office. I kissed his hand again and, calling on God to take care of him, I left.

The office of the Salesians was near the new and very modern traffic circle in the heart of Warsaw. The priest on duty greeted me in the name of God and asked me the reason for my visit. I gave him a short version of my history, but refused the temptation to replace Piotr Grodzieński with Arthur Ney. Blaming the authorities, the priest said that they had barely been able to accommodate all the boys they had lodged during the occupation, much less take on any new ones. The order had been obliged to direct new orphans to government-run orphanages. He scribbled the name and address of the Salesian institution outside Warsaw and told me to take the train to Głosków, one station south of Szczaki, the station nearest Runów; from there, he said, any passerby would give me directions to the orphanage. I felt as if I was going home and wondered what mysterious forces had been guiding my steps.

It was getting late in the day and I had no further interest in staying in Warsaw. In my mind, I was already planning my visit to Runów and seeing the Puchała family again. I thanked the priest, said goodbye and hurried to the same narrow-gauge train station that some months before I had used to go from Warsaw to Runów and back.

In Szczaki, as the priest had said, a station employee pointed out the cluster of houses that made up the orphanage. Once at the institution, I was guided to the priest-director, registered and shown where I would sleep and where supper would be served. The main building of the orphanage housed a chapel, the dormitories and shower rooms, and there were toilets on both the first and second floors. The refectory, which also served as a study hall and recreation room, was on the ground floor, as were the sleeping quarters for the ordained priests, who were also the administrators. The rector, Father Ignaczewski, had an office there.

There were about twenty-five boys in the orphanage, three administrators, and three seminarians. The start of the school year was approaching and a few days after my arrival, Father Ignaczewski sent me to register at a renowned *gimnazjum* named Emilia Plater, known to everyone by its diminutive, Plateruwka. A *gimnazjum* was a purely academic high school; upon completion of its three- or four-year program, it offered a diploma called a *metryka* that could lead to university. The school was co-ed but not the classes, and, as elsewhere, the boys studied English as a foreign language, while the girls French. Russian was not yet compulsory.

Life in the orphanage was based on a very simple schedule because of the limited resources. The days were somewhat different for me than they were for the other boys since I was the oldest and the only one attending *gimnazjum*. I ate breakfast with the rest of the boys, but I missed lunch, which meant that I had to fast most of the day, only eating supper with the other boys when I returned from school in the afternoon. On the days when I was able to return from Plateruwka earlier, I joined the others to do homework in the refectory before supper. On Saturdays, we worked on the farm and played at least one outdoor game. On Sundays, we attended mass in the chapel, along with many local peasants who, since there was very little space, had to stand in the entrance hall and on the staircase. On Sunday afternoons, there were usually a few relatives who visited the boys. I found Sunday afternoons difficult for this reason, but I wasn't the only boy without visitors.

School had started September 1, 1945, the sixth anniversary of the German invasion of Poland. From the very beginning, under tremendous pressure from the Soviets, the authorities slowly but surely forced many schools like ours to introduce lectures promoting communism. At the same time, they limited religious and Polish-cultural influence by forbidding lessons in Polish history and the teaching of literature about Polish national heroes. On one occasion, Polish authorities accompanied by Soviet officers and party members came to Plateruwka and physically removed the Polish national emblem, the crowned eagle, from every wall. There was no violent resistance to this move but there was collective booing in every classroom where this was done, despite angry looks from the Soviets.

My life became highly disciplined, divided as it was between the orphanage and the *gimnazjum*. I had good relationships with the priests and the professors and managed to form a small group of friends at both places, partly because we all took the same train and got off and on at the same stations. Among them were Fredek Marcinkowski, Janusz Żurkowski, and, to our delight, Danuta Kowalefska, the most beautiful girl in the school (although she unfortunately was dating an older student).

One day, when Danuta failed to show up at the train station or at school, Fredek, Janusz and I each started to investigate what had happened to her without discussing it with each other. When I found out that she had just undergone an emergency appendectomy, I was determined to visit her in the hospital and perhaps even take her flowers. In the speech that I would have to make to Father Ignaczewski to ask for permission and money for a train ticket, I planned to point out that the catechism I had learned in 1943 had taught me that visiting the sick was a Work of Mercy. As I stood at attention delivering my well-prepared plea, I saw the priest's eyes start to twinkle. He pulled a few złotys from his desk drawer and, looking straight into my eyes, recited a famous Polish proverb: "A boy who brings flowers is either stupid or innocent." I hoped he meant the latter and beat a quick retreat before he could change his mind.

Putting Father Ignaczewski's proverb out of my mind, I bought a big bouquet of flowers and, with my heart pounding and hands sweating, I went into Danuta's hospital room. I couldn't believe my eyes. On each side of her bed, their flowers forming a frame around her head, sat Fredek and Janusz staring at me in astonishment. They had beaten me to it. As if on command, all four of us burst into uncontrollable laughter, which immediately brought the sister rushing into the room and threatening all three of us with expulsion. This episode became known to our whole school, students and teacher alike, and for weeks afterward, all four of us were subjected to meaningful looks and chuckles.

～

I continued to live as a Christian under my wartime pseudonym, Piotr Grodzieński. The priests knew that I was Jewish but they didn't treat me any differently. On the contrary, knowing that I had been baptized – although this had been done to save my life – Father Ignaczewski sometimes had me serve him mass when he and I had to catch the same early train. He went to Warsaw and I stopped at the station serving Plateruwka.

One day, before the beginning of a class, our homeroom teacher said in a very official tone that he had been told by the authorities to ask a certain question. Using the most diplomatic formulation imaginable, he asked if there was anyone in class of the "Mosaic persuasion." The old feeling of insecurity immediately rose up in me. So far, no one in the school knew I was Jewish. I avoided meeting the teacher's eyes because I knew that if our eyes met, even for a second, I would give myself away. I dove under my desk and started tying and untying my shoelaces, wishing I could become invisible. After what seemed like an eternity, during which no one pronounced himself Jewish, the teacher carried on as usual. I, however, became fearful and nervous. I didn't realize it at the time, but this was the beginning of my dissatisfaction with living under an assumed identity and a longing to resume being Artur Ney.

Despite these feelings, I look back on this period as having been a happy time in my life. I was well treated both at school and the orphanage. We didn't have enough to eat, nor did we have enough clothing, but we felt that the administration was doing its best for us, especially the rector, Father Ignaczewski. He was the ambassador between the bureaucratic government and the orphanage, and was constantly travelling to Warsaw to visit government institutions that distributed food and clothes, usually provided to poor people and orphanages by international organizations.

From time to time, he asked me to accompany him to help transport these contributions. To my surprise, the government employees we had to deal with to get these provisions were Jewish and made no effort to hide the fact. Most of them had survived the war by escaping to the Soviet Union and had returned as soldiers. There were sometimes heated exchanges between Father Ignaczewski and these civil servants – Father Ignaczewski wore his cassock, as if to emphasize his religious identity and provoke a negative reaction. When I accompanied him, I had the feeling that these civil servants suspected that I was Jewish.

I knew that Jewish scouts were crisscrossing Poland, trying to identify Jewish children who had been given to gentile Poles by

Jewish parents to save the child's life. There were many tragic scenes in which the children, unaware of their Jewish identity, were torn away from the only parents they knew. The majority of these children were girls, since circumcision, if discovered, would have condemned any Jewish boy along with his adoptive parents. At that moment, I was not ready to "come out of the closet." The problem of my identity was swirling around my consciousness like a gathering storm. I was simultaneously preoccupied with my future and coming to terms with my past – in particular, with the loss of my family.

One day, Father Ignaczewski told me that he needed to send me alone to Praga with two horses and a wagon. He may have felt that since I was Jewish, I would be treated better and get more and better food for the orphanage. Father Ignaczewski had given me general directions to Praga and told me that once there, I would have to ask for further directions. Even he was not sure of the route because of constant reconstruction and repair work in the streets. Had I read the address of my destination in advance, something would have clicked in my head but I didn't.

The trip to Warsaw took several hours and, being market day, there were many farmers and wagons on the roads. I finally crossed the bridge from Warsaw, pulled my wagon to a stop near the sidewalk and reached for the paper with the name of the street where I had to go. As I read the address I began to shake. The street on which the distribution centre was located was 11 Listopada, Eleventh of November, and the centre was at No. 9. The address of my family's dry cleaning plant had been No. 10, Eleventh of November Street. My imagination went wild and I saw scenes with my mother, Aunt Ronia and some of the plant workers.

I don't remember how long I stayed there, but eventually I asked passersby for the shortest route to my destination. I was overwhelmed with excitement. I drove the horses to Eleventh of November Street and soon I was facing the courtyard of No. 10. I stared at our former plant and my heart sank. It was clearly empty and the windows were too dirty for me to see inside. I tried to open the door but it was locked – another disappointment. The dream of seeing my mother, Ronia and their workers evaporated. I realized that I had always remembered this place, but had not been able to face visiting it, for such a visit could only confirm that my whole family had perished.

Then it happened, the event that determined the rest of my life. A woman was standing in another part of the courtyard, in front of a neighbouring building, chopping wood. As I was about to go out into the street, something made me stop. I turned back toward the woman and asked her awkwardly if by some chance she knew whether anyone from the Holcman family had survived. If so, did she have any idea where they were? To my astonishment, the woman straightened up, let the huge axe slip from her hands and, after calling on every saint in Christendom, cried out, "Turek! Tureczek!"

She put her arms around me and continued to cry out my name. Disoriented, I repeated my question, not recognizing the woman despite her obvious familiarity with me. She realized that I was at a loss and told me her name was Irka, that she had been one of the foreladies at the plant. She tightened her grip on my shoulder and, looking into my eyes as if for assurance that what she was about to say would be understood, she triumphantly announced that Ronia and her husband, Józiek, had survived, that Ronia had visited her a few days after the liberation of Warsaw. Most importantly, Irka said that my aunt had left her current address in Pruszków, not far from Warsaw.

Irka invited me upstairs to her apartment to eat something and answer the millions of questions she had for me. The visit was wonderful and filled with emotion on both sides. I told her how I had miraculously survived since my family had abandoned the Praga plant in late 1940. I left Irka my address at the orphanage, got Ronia's Pruszków address from her and promised to stay in touch. Then I took my leave and went next door to the distribution centre. How differently I felt from former occasions when I had had to "go to the

Jews," as the Poles said, to collect food or clothes. The previous times I had entered those centres feeling timid and guilty because I did not declare to these civil servants that I was Jewish, though their manner had invited me to. This time, I entered the premises with my head held high, sure of myself. When I felt their demanding eyes on me, instead of turning away or looking down, I gazed directly at them, as if my eyes could say, "Leave me alone; the game is over. I will tell you I'm Jewish when I'm ready." Although I hadn't found them yet, my aunt and uncle, whom I loved like my parents, had survived! I was no longer alone in the world and my beloved relatives would eventually take care of me.

I arrived back at the orphanage late the same evening. To my disappointment, it was too late to see Father Ignaczewski and it was another few days before the busy rector granted me an audience. I was able to tell him my exciting story in a calmer frame of mind than would have been possible if I had seen him immediately. In the meantime, negative feelings made me imagine his refusal to help me find my relatives. After a few minutes, though, I realized that my fears were groundless. Father Ignaczewski not only agreed to help me but also gave me a small sum of money for my trip to Pruszków. I didn't share my news with anyone else at school or the orphanage.

The change in me must have been noticeable, for my friends in Plateruwka and at home looked at me curiously. Finally the long-awaited day arrived. I took the same morning train to Warsaw that I took to school every day, since I had to pass through Warsaw to get to Pruszków. I arrived at the Pruszków station and received directions to the address Ronia had given Irka. From that moment until I knocked at Ronia's door, my heart was in my mouth and my stomach full of the familiar butterflies.

Finding Family

When the door opened at Ronia and Józiek's house I saw only a middle-aged woman I didn't know. However, my disappointment gave way to a more hopeful feeling when, as she listened to my story, the woman smiled and nodded encouragingly. She said that Ronia and Józiek had lived in her apartment during the war while she was a slave labourer in Germany. Her sister Nacia had met them in the prisoner-of-war camp in Pruszków, where Warsaw civilians had been sent for "sorting" into slave labourers destined for Germany after the uprising.

Nacia, Ronia and Józiek had escaped to the town, where Nacia allowed Ronia and Józiek to occupy her sister's empty apartment. She added that she didn't know where my aunt and uncle were now, but perhaps Nacia did. She gave me her address and said that my uncle had worked at the Pruszków city hall immediately after the war. As though she only half believed it, she also added that Józiek was a general in the army. Nacia, she said, would be working until 5:00 p.m. that day.

When Nacia arrived home, I told her that Ronia and Józiek had been friends with my parents, and since I was now an orphan, living in an orphanage, I was desperately looking for anyone who had known my family. Instinct told me not to say that we were related or that they were married to each other since I didn't want to disclose that any of us were Jewish. It turned out later to have been prudent to hide these facts – Nacia believed that they were Christian Poles who were not married to each other.

Nacia invited me in and offered me a very welcome bowl of soup. She explained how she had met Ronia and Józiek, and how they had planned and executed their escape from the prisoner-of-war camp. She also described the constant fear that all three of them had lived with after their escape near the end of 1944, until liberation in early 1945. It was a blessing that her sister's apartment was empty because if she had gone back to her own apartment with two extra people, it would have attracted unwanted attention.

Nacia summed up what she knew about my aunt and uncle, which was very little. She said nothing about my uncle being a general in the army. Ronia and Józiek had apparently moved to Lodz, about two hours by train from Warsaw, shortly after liberation, but had not left their address because they didn't know how long they would be staying there. Nevertheless, she added, Józiek had promised to come back to visit her from time to time.

I decided that I should leave a clue to my whereabouts with Nacia without disclosing who I really was or my relationship to my aunt and uncle. I wrote on a piece of paper "Piotr Grodzieński, c/o the Salesian Fathers' Orphanage, Zielone, Głosków." Then I added the two letters "A.N." I thanked my lucky stars that Nacia didn't ask me the meaning of this postscript, for I have no idea how I would have answered her. As it turned out, this was the information that my aunt and uncle absolutely needed to find me, the only clue they would have that I was still alive. They had never known my pseudonym or even that I had one.

During the train ride back to the orphanage I felt hopeless at the prospect of finding Ronia and Józiek. The next day, I asked Father Ignaczewski for some writing paper and wrote a short note, addressed "To whom it may concern," explaining that I was looking for my uncle who, according to information that I had received, was a general in the army. I addressed the envelope to the Polish General Army Command, Personal Research Division in Lodz.

~

On a grey, windy afternoon in the fall of 1946, while I was doing homework with the other boys in the refectory, I put down my pen and looked around at the faces of the other boys and the priest reading his breviary. By now, we were enjoying the golden Polish autumn – the leaves continued to change colours before they fell in greater and greater numbers; the farmers' fields had been cleared after the harvest and haystacks had appeared in place of the crops. I could see the falling leaves through the single-paned windows and heard the wind howling.

In front of me lay an official letter from the Polish General Army Command Personal Research Division and for the tenth time, I read its terse message. Much to their regret, there was no record of a General Józef Borzewski in any section of the Polish army, including veterans. Wishing me luck and promising to help in any other search, the letter was signed by an officer in the Polish army.

The more I looked around me, the more I felt that I had to do something about the way I was feeling and about my future. Otherwise, I would be paralyzed, unable to carry on. I was living with the constant fear that my true identity would be unmasked, and because of it there could be no true comradeship between me and my peers. Even my relationships to the priests who ran the orphanage were artificial. I was hungry for news about the few Polish Jewish survivors who had emerged from hiding places and concentration camps, as well as those who had returned from the Soviet Union. But I had to be careful not to arouse suspicion about my true identity.

I was also becoming increasingly conscious of my rapidly maturing body. I attended a co-ed high school and even though contact with the girls was minimal, I often fantasized about them. I couldn't bring myself to discuss these thoughts with my friends from Plateruwka or with my fellow orphans, much less with the priests. Talking about puberty would lead, I had heard, to comparing the development of our genitals; in my case, that would be disastrous. This was the state of mind I was in when I wrote the first page of my diary, which, more than sixty years later, evolved into this memoir. The priest's loud clapping interrupted my reverie and brought me back to the present. He announced that it was the end of study period and the beginning of the next activity in our highly disciplined life.

~

One day after school, Fredek and I decided to walk home along the railway track rather than take the short train ride. I no longer remember what we were talking about, but the time passed quickly and we soon arrived at the crossroads where Fredek would turn right and I would turn left. As we stood at the intersection, I looked toward the orphanage – it was completely visible because the land was flat and the fields empty – and couldn't believe my eyes. Although I hadn't seen him since 1942, there could be no possible mistake. Standing in front of the main building, talking to the Father Director, was my uncle Józiek, wearing the kind of winter coat with a beautiful fur collar that he had always worn.

Stuttering and hesitating, I turned to Fredek and croaked, "That's my uncle!" I started to run across the fields. We were only a few hundred metres away and the closer I got the more excited I became. The man was indeed Uncle Józiek. He had obviously received the note that I had left with Nacia and interpreted it correctly. We didn't embrace, or shake hands; neither of us showed any deep emotion because we were inhibited by the priest's presence. Nevertheless, I felt that my need for someone to replace my parents was going to be fulfilled at last.

The Father Director granted me permission to leave with Uncle Józiek. Feeling like a bird just released from its cage, I ran upstairs to my locker to get my one extra pair of socks and shirt. I was too overwhelmed with emotion to find my friends and say goodbye. I ran back to my uncle and the Father Director, who were still talking outside the main building. Józiek shook the priest's hand, Piotr Grodzieński kissed that same hand, and Arthur Ney entered his new life.

Józiek wanted to travel to Lodz immediately so I could be reunited with Aunt Ronia as soon as possible. He predicted that she would be waiting for me at the door to the stairwell, listening avidly to every sound from outside. We would first take the narrow-gauge train from Głosków, linking with the regular train at Piaseczno and from there go on to Warsaw, where we would change trains for the last leg of our journey. Even though I realized that we were hours from our destination, the thought of seeing Ronia again made me feel restless with excitement. When the narrow-gauge train arrived, it was as usual packed beyond capacity, and there was hardly any standing room.

As the train started to move, I glanced back across the empty fields at the orphanage for the last time. It's hard to describe my feelings at that moment. The best I can do is to say that my pleasant memories of the place were mixed with my ambivalence about the need for me to keep my secret.

The crowding on the train and Józiek's unhappiness about the food odours as well as the unpleasant smells of body odour, tobacco, vodka and, worst of all, bad breath increased as we approached Piaseczno. At the sight of more passengers getting on there, he decided that we had to find a new means of transportation. We ended up standing on the street outside the station, where there were few passersby and I wondered what my uncle expected to find in the gathering darkness.

Suddenly, a black limousine with Polish and Soviet flags attached to the hood ornament drove up slowly, looking for a place to park. When he saw the car, to my astonishment Józiek exclaimed, "For the last leg of our journey, we will drive in style!" We crossed the road and my uncle approached the limousine driver. The Polish driver worked for a limousine service for diplomats but this was his day off and he had come to visit his relatives in Piaseczno. After a bit of bargaining, the man accepted payment to drive us to Lodz. I found myself sitting in the plush back seat of the limousine, staring out at the night as we passed through the countryside. I was drunk with happiness and light-headed at the fast pace of all the change. Most of all, I was thrilled at the thought that I would soon be reunited with Aunt Ronia.

When we stopped in front of my aunt and uncle's place, Józiek pulled the bell cord to wake up the janitor so he could open the gate to the courtyard and staircase to their apartment. Bundled in his winter clothes and muttering under his breath in terms that were not complimentary to my uncle, the unhappy janitor reluctantly opened the gate, bowing to us when Józiek pushed a folded bill into his hand.

I trembled with excitement as we climbed the stairs. On one of the landings, my uncle stopped and whispered, "Ronia is surely waiting at the door and I would like to prepare her a little so she won't faint." He had started ahead when we heard a door open noisily and hit the wall without any regard for sleeping neighbours. In a flash my aunt was running down the stairs, screaming at Józiek, "Where is Artur? Where is Turek? Why didn't he come with you?" This was too much for me. I ran up the steps two at a time and grabbed my tiny, skinny aunt. For some time, we stood silently, neither of us able to speak. Then we all went into the apartment, asking each other the same questions over and over. It was well into the morning when we finally went to bed.

As I lay awake, too excited to sleep, it dawned on me that it was a miracle that I had made contact with my uncle and aunt, who it turned out were planning to immigrate to Canada in a few months. It was just a coincidence that the distribution centre was located beside our dry cleaning plant and that Irka happened to be in the courtyard when I came. It also was miraculous that my uncle had decided to go back to Pruszków to say goodbye to Nacia before leaving for Canada and received the note that I had left for them.

The next few days were filled with more questions and answers, more tears and embraces. I followed my aunt everywhere she went. Józiek insisted I have several irons in the fire regarding my future. Because it was not definite that we could immigrate to Canada, he took me to register in a Jewish organization that was preparing to send a group of orphaned Jewish children and teenagers to France. At the same time, he sent special delivery letters to Canada and New York. Ronia and I were related to a well-to-do and influential family in Montreal and Ronia also had a brother in New York who had left Poland in his early teens, before she was born, and was now a successful businessman. Our cousins in Montreal, whose father had been the man my parents had stayed with in Bialystok all those years ago, agreed to sponsor all three of us for immigration to Canada and started the application process. Meanwhile, they sent us money through the mail, which had recently started functioning more reliably. In preparation for my departure for France, my uncle used the money to outfit me with the first set of fine clothes that I had had since childhood.

I began to follow a new routine. In the morning, I joined the other Jewish orphans leaving for France to learn about what was then known as British Mandate Palestine – the future State of Israel. We also learned basic Hebrew. During these sessions I met Piotr Ruff, who became a classmate in France and a lifelong friend, although our paths were to later diverge. In the afternoon, I returned to our freezing apartment – there was no heating at all – and remained behind the closed double iron doors that my uncle had installed.

Józiek and Ronia were still living under their assumed Polish names – Borzewski and Wendrychowska – and my uncle pretended to be a single man living with his late friend's widow. Although the war had been over for a year and a half and, supposedly, antisemitism was officially not tolerated in Poland, Jews continued to live in fear. This fear was justified by the infamous Kielce pogrom that had been perpetrated shortly before I arrived in Lodz. Józiek kept a loaded German Luger carefully hidden.

At the beginning of 1947, I unexpectedly received a notice from the organization in charge of my group giving me a date for my departure to France, a date that allowed us only a few weeks to prepare. It had been months since I left the orphanage and I often thought about the people who had been in my life for a year and a half, friends from both the high school and the institution. My imminent departure suddenly made me realize how attached I had become to my former life there.

I tried to dispel my sadness by writing a letter to my classmate and dear friend Fredek, telling him that I would be coming to see Danuta, Janusz and him and that I would meet them at the train station in Danuta's village. When I took the same narrow-gauge train that I had taken so many times between the orphanage and the *gimnazjum*, many different thoughts and emotions went through my mind. I felt particularly sad that despite our sincere friendship I was, to them, still Piotr Grodzieński. My real name, life history and identity remained secret from them until I returned to Poland in 1988.

We all met at the train station and went to Danuta's house. It was a very happy event, during which I took the liberty of placing a tiny kiss on Danuta's lips. Everyone applauded, Danuta laughed demurely and I was in seventh heaven. After I had promised to write from Canada, my three friends walked me back to the station, where there were handshakes, hugs, and more kisses for Danuta. Piotr Grodzieński then turned, climbed into the train and disappeared.

I fully realized that I was closing one in a series of doors in my tragic and turbulent young life. Reflecting on why I never went back to visit the farm village of Runów or the orphanage in Głosków to say goodbye despite my warm feelings for people in both places who had helped me, I realize that it was because some of them had known that I was Jewish. It was possible that some were beginning to feel the impact of dealing with Jewish civil servants who had returned to Poland with the Soviet army. I couldn't bear the thought of a possible random reprisal against me for want of a more appropriate target. I also wanted to obliterate the trail of Piotr Grodzieński/Artur Ney in Poland.

Ronia, Józiek and I now began the hectic preparations for my departure. My aunt and uncle sent letters to all my relatives outside Poland, notifying them of my departure for France. Ronia issued a litany of things not to do during the trip – she urged me to stop bothering young girls, for example, a piece of advice I had no intention of following. The day finally arrived and we loaded my beautiful new leather suitcase filled with new custom-made clothes into a taxi. I carried a knapsack on my back containing my personal papers, including the first pages of the first version of this memoir.

I joined my group, including the adults who would serve as armed guards in case we encountered trouble, on the platform at the train station. All the guards were Jewish and wore civilian clothes with their weapons concealed under their winter coats. When I arrived with Ronia and Józiek, a redcap put my suitcase into a special freight car guarded by a uniformed Polish militia man. Just before departure, the car was padlocked and its key given to the director of our group.

Then came the "all aboard!" and the last kisses and hugs with relatives and friends. I stood by the closed window and watched the station receding into the distance with mixed feelings. As the train picked up speed, I listened to the noise of the wheels on the tracks and looked at the houses and villages flashing by. For the first time since I had been reunited with Ronia and Józiek, I started to cry. I saw myself standing with my mother in the *Umschlagplatz*, in the next foursome waiting for a sign from the German officer stationed at the half-closed freight car door to come forward and be sent to our deaths.

The happy sounds of young people visiting each other's compartments woke me out of this nightmare. Some, having spent most of their wartime lives in hiding, had never been on a train before. One of the cars had been transformed into a dining room and we all gathered there for a meal and were given our itinerary for the first time.

The first stop would be Prague, where we would leave the train for a short time and stay in barracks specially built for us and other groups who would follow. In Prague we would be issued legal documents and then resume our journey to France.

When we arrived in the station in Prague, the director unlocked the luggage car and nominated three or four young adults to place all the luggage on the platform for identification. As I waited patiently for my suitcase to appear, the crowd started to thin out and, finally, I was the only one left standing in front of the now-empty baggage car. I argued with the young men acting as porters, telling them that they had somehow misplaced my suitcase. They invited me to come in and check the car for myself, but, unnerved by the prospect of going into a freight car, I refused.

Understanding my reluctance, the director offered to search for me and emerged shortly after empty-handed, looking sympathetic. I realized that the Polish porters who had loaded the car through one door must have managed to push my suitcase out the other side. With my valuable new leather suitcase, I was the only one who was robbed. The director reported the theft to the Czech authorities and we went to our barracks for our ten-day stay in Prague. Almost every day, our guides led us to different parts of Prague. We saw world-famous buildings, museums, churches and one or two surviving synagogues.

Our brief sojourn as tourists passed quickly and the time came to move on. The train from Prague also carried ordinary civilians and military personnel. Most of us stared out the windows at the snow-covered countryside as it raced by and I did the same, lost in thought. From the day I left the orphanage with my uncle, events had moved quickly. Except for the theft of my suitcase, everything was now going in a positive direction. However, every time my thoughts strayed to the war it was as if a gate opened up to let a flood of pessimism wash over me. Memories of my lost family and the tragic events I had lived through prevented me from fully enjoying my new freedom and security.

The adults escorting us had assured us that we would no longer have to struggle for survival, that our future would be taken care of as long as we continued our education. Our supervisors, who were also our teachers, had started instructing us in Hebrew while we were still in Poland, beginning with songs. They taught us the history of ancient Palestine, where the Jewish people had lived, and about the succession of monarchies, including the reign of King David. I was impressed with the history and the famous battles that the Jews had won in Palestine. I began looking forward to speaking Hebrew and singing Hebrew songs.

Even though I was only sixteen, I recognized that our teachers were trying to help us forget the past as subtly as possible and to plant Zionist idealism in our minds. They described life on the kibbutzim in a positive, desirable light. Yet, all this time, I was still sure that I was going to Canada, a country I knew nothing about. I felt like a long-distance runner who was nearing the finish line, breathless but filled with the excitement of victory.

The train stopped at the Gare de l'Est in Paris and as people poured onto the platform, our group hastily assembled with our supervisors. I admired the job that our organizers had done in achieving this exodus – not only had they taken us out of Egypt, but they had also led us, if not to the Promised Land, then to an oasis on the way to it.

When I opened my hotel room window, the warm spring air filled with fragrances from flowers to motorcycle fuel washed over me. From the street, the shouts of the city assaulted my ears and I couldn't understand a single word, so I shut the window, pulled down the shutters, undressed and collapsed into bed. I slept for the next seventeen hours, until 10:00 a.m. the next morning. That was how I spent my first night in Paris.

During breakfast, the director announced that we would be leaving Paris before noon in a chartered bus that would take us to our final destination. There were loud voices of protest, but I knew this decision was irreversible. As promised, a huge, solid-looking and extremely comfortable bus arrived for us shortly before noon. There was enough room for everyone, with ample space for luggage. I was the only person in the group whose baggage could be held in one hand.

After a few hours steadily climbing to higher altitudes in the region of the Massif Central, we drove through uninhabited countryside surrounded by beautiful but unfamiliar bushes and trees. The kids were enthusiastic about the prospect of living in the wilderness and playing cowboys and Indians, but the adults openly expressed concern about being so far from civilization. Then, in this middle of nowhere, a multi-storey building surrounded by half a dozen cottages appeared. This tiny settlement was in turn encircled by farmland with grazing animals and growing crops. What excited me most was the flock of sheep, an animal that I knew only from pictures.

This was the Château de Montintin, the end of the line for this phase of our journey. Despite its apparent isolation, this small château was in fact near Limoges. It had been used by the L'Œuvre de Secours aux Enfants (OSE), to hide Jewish children during the war; after the war, Jewish organizations had either rented or bought the property from the French government to use for preparing groups like ours for immigration to British Mandate Palestine. When it was no longer needed for that purpose, it was used as a summer camp for Jews from Paris and the vicinity until its reversion to the descendants of its original owners.

Soon after our arrival, we were shown to our rooms and given a tour of the premises and surrounding cottages that served as private rooms for the staff. The director of the Château was a medical doctor who, with his wife, occupied a small apartment in the main building. Our teacher-guards, under the guidance of the group commander, were very well organized and from about the third day on, we kept to a routine that stayed the same during the whole time that I was there.

Our day started with an outdoor gym session, followed by a healthy French-style breakfast. We then took classes in conversational Hebrew and in the geography and history of the region of Palestine from ancient to modern times. Wall maps showed the location of the country in relation to the seas, mountains and neighbouring Arab lands – for many of us, this was the first time that we saw what would become the State of Israel as a separate country.

Piotr Ruff and I became close friends at the Château – I liked him from the start but admit that I was a little jealous of him. Although the Nazis had killed his father, he was not an orphan and corresponded regularly with his mother in Poland. Piotr taught me to play chess and also sometimes played with Krysia, the younger sister of an adult staff member. Krysia reciprocated Piotr's interest in her, but I wasn't jealous of that – I was too busy flirting with several other girls in the group.

Piotr jogged every day on the narrow path between the trees and bushes surrounding our settlement and one day asked me to join him, assuring me that it would put me in shape. I took up the challenge, but he very soon outdistanced me and I began to feel tired, out of breath and afraid of collapsing. I yelled at him to stop and wait for me but Piotr insisted that if I continued, I would get my second wind. His speech boosted my morale and we started up again; I indeed did feel a renewed energy. This incident made me respect Piotr even more and remember the lesson of forging ahead in the face of exhaustion, anticipating a second wind.

Piotr and I were about the same age and often talked about our physical maturation. Not long after one of these discussions, as though he had heard us talking, our group director presented both of us with shaving kits. The first few times we tried to shave we had to apply iodine to our sideburns, but within a week or so, the younger boys were jealous of us.

By now, none of us had any doubts about our final destination. Not only did we not object to being taken to pre-state Israel, but we were eager to learn anything we might be able to use there, from cooking to nursing. Piotr and I were the only boys old enough to be introduced to arms and military equipment. We wanted to improve our skills in target-practice, knowing that our teachers had brought guns with them, but they reminded us that we were in a foreign country and any shooting would create immense problems. The director promised, however, to bring to camp members of the Haganah, the Jewish paramilitary force, who would teach us the art of self-defence without weapons.

We were taught how to defend ourselves against the clubs carried by British soldiers, who used the weapons to disperse demonstrations. We were each given a thick stick similar to the British clubs and were taught to hold it in front of our faces with both hands and our arms slightly bent. The stick was held roughly parallel to the ground and perpendicular to the stroke of the club coming at us so that the descending club would hit the defending stick and absorb most of the shock. This way, the reverberating shock often caused more pain to the attackers than to the defenders. It was especially interesting to watch how successfully our instructors defended themselves when we played the role of the attackers. We often continued practising after the instruction was over.

My list of correspondents had grown considerably in the period since my uncle took me from the orphanage. I of course wrote to Ronia and Józiek, who by now were living in Paris, in the hotel where our group had spent its one night. I was also now corresponding with my father's sister in Palestine; a branch of my father's large family in Canada; my father's brother Stach in Vienna; and two more distant relatives from the Ney side who had lived in Paris since before the war.

My cousins in Canada assured me that it was only a matter of time and formalities before I would be able to immigrate there, which made the others envious of me. Everyone thought that immigrating to North America was like going to Paradise.

In contrast to this abundance of family on my father's side, I only knew of one cousin on my mother's side who had survived, having escaped to the Soviet Union in 1939 – Janek, who was Uncle Kuba's son and my cousin Stach's brother. I had to assume that Stach had perished in Warsaw since we hadn't heard anything from him after we left the hiding place in Dr. Płocker's apartment in 1942. Janek graduated from the Moscow Conservatory and became a renowned and decorated pianist. He later immigrated to the United States, where he published a book on the composer Chopin. Totally disillusioned by life in New York, however, he committed suicide in the late 1950s. I was never able to find any other surviving members of my mother's family.

I was happy during my time at the Château, yet I knew that I was not in control of the coming changes in my life. The uncertainty of a future that lay in the hands of Canadian relatives I had never met made me apprehensive.

In the summer of 1947 the crops in the fields around the Château were maturing but not yet harvested and the panorama of colours changed daily. On one of those warm, colourful summer days I received a letter from Ronia and Józiek telling me that I had an appointment at the Canadian consulate in Paris and had to get there as soon as possible. After kissing the girls, shakings hands with the boys and men and promising Piotr that we would stay in touch, I said goodbye to the director. He knew that I was feeling guilty about leaving for North America while the rest of our group was going to carry on the fight for our homeland. He broke off a small branch from a nearby bush, drew a circle around him in the sand, then stepped out of the circle and pointed to it with the stick. "By turning constantly to the left or to the right," he said, "you will eventually end up at your starting point." He was predicting that having come this far, I would one day end up in the land of Israel. After finishing his prophecy, he shook my hand, wished me luck and asked me to stay in touch. I got on the bus, waved goodbye to my friends and, fighting tears, stared back at the Château disappearing in the distance.

The Decision

As the bus took me away from the Château and even farther from the life I had known, I stretched my legs onto the seat opposite, loosened my belt and let my mind wander. As had happened throughout the last few years, I fell into the trap of thinking about my family and their fate. Logic told me to accept that they couldn't possibly have survived since I would have found them by now. My illogical side, however, constantly forced me to hope and dream that they were still alive somewhere. The image of my sister came to me. I had adored her and always obeyed her blindly. Accepting her death was too painful to bear. As I had before, I imagined ways that she might have escaped – in this fantasy I saw a German officer falling in love with her and marrying her, taking her away to a place where she had decided to live without ever disclosing her Jewish origins.

When I realized that we were in Paris, I grabbed my rucksack and prepared to be dropped at the hotel on the rue Château d'Eau. This time I was assigned a small room in the attic, with a large window looking out onto roofs and balconies of the nearby buildings. Ronia and Józiek were staying on a lower floor of the same hotel. From my window, I watched the daily activities of ordinary Parisians, which, in fine weather, took place on balconies and rooftops. On sunny days, the sun poured in to my west-facing room for most of the afternoon. I could hear the Montmartre-inspired accordionists, although I couldn't see them from my window.

The first few days after my arrival were spent registering as a foreigner in France and acquiring all sorts of documents that were necessary to get rationed food and other necessities even as a refugee in transit. I had to go to the Canadian consulate to submit my immigration application, sponsored by my Canadian relatives. At this point I ran into a new problem – the process of obtaining all the necessary papers would take several months but I couldn't legally stay in Paris without working and I couldn't legally work without a residence permit for Paris. The solution came from my father's cousin Maurice Ney who ran a small knitting factory with his brother Henri. I was able to acquire a certificate of employment through Maurice, which enabled me to get permission to live and work in Paris. I did in fact work for Maurice while I was in Paris and it was my first real job. I was finally able to support myself, a fact of which I was very proud.

Maurice and Henri Ney had come to Paris from the small Polish town of Sandomierz well before the war. During the war, Maurice married a Christian woman, the beautiful and charming Morisette, who helped save his life, and they had a little girl. I have remained in touch with this family ever since, although now it is with Maurice and Morisette's children. Henri, on the other hand, had been in the French army at the start of the war and was single. He later married and had a son, but I lost contact with him.

While I stayed in Paris I worked at Maurice's factory all day. Henri and I, the only workers, were in charge of manufacturing garments and Maurice administered the business, which included seeing clients. In the late afternoons and evenings, I went for walks with Ronia and Józiek. I met other young people in similar circumstances to mine, waiting to immigrate to various countries. I attended a crash course in French given through one of the several Jewish organizations in Paris. And, for the first time in my life, I started dating girls.

Out shopping in a pharmacy with Józiek and Ronia, I noticed that one of the clerks was a pretty redhead and, to my astonishment, she said a few words to me in Polish, for she had heard us talking among ourselves. I clumsily began a conversation and when she encouraged me, I lost my inhibitions. I wanted to ask her out and knew if I didn't do it right away, I would miss my chance. To my astonishment, she accepted and gave me her telephone number. I began calling her every day and eventually, the date was set. It was agreed that we would go dancing, for that was what she loved to do. I hung the phone up and panicked – I had no idea how to dance. The concierge had heard my conversation, but hadn't understood a word since he didn't speak Polish. Nevertheless, he guessed that I had been making a date.

Turning toward me with a straight face, he said, "L'amour, l'amour, toujours l'amour!" (Love, love, love forever!) Using my ever-present dictionary, I looked up the necessary words to ask the concierge how I could learn to dance. He answered my cry for help speaking slowly and carefully, and supplemented his answer with gestures. What I understood was that he was suggesting dancing lessons in a school that turned out to be only a block away. Work the next day dragged on mercilessly and at 4:00 p.m., I raced to the dance studio. Unfortunately a notice on the door said that the school was closed for the vacation period. Seeing my dismay, the storekeeper next door began speaking in what was to me incomprehensible French. He rang the doorbell of the dancing school and, sure enough, there was an answering buzz to let me in. With repeated cries of "merci!" to the shopkeeper, I went inside.

Pulling out my dictionary again, I explained my predicament to the dance school proprietor and it took about an hour of broken dictionary French for us to understand each other. There was no female dance teacher available since all were on vacation, but this gentleman, being the owner, was willing to teach me how to dance. I accepted his offer, gave him a deposit for a crash course and went home dreaming about my red-haired beauty.

The dance lessons went very well and I became more confident of my hidden talents. I practised in my tiny room, whistling the tunes from the dance school and the fateful day finally arrived. The redhead and I met at a three-storey building with a dance hall on each floor and three different orchestras. To say that I was nervous as we stood waiting for the music to begin would be an understatement. When it did start, thanks to my lessons I recognized that it was a well-known tango. To dance the tango properly, you have to start on a certain beat. I put my arms where I had been told to and tried to pick out the starting beat. Couples around us, who were already dancing, looked at me and laughed, which made things worse.

Then mercifully the music stopped. My date asked me straight out if I had ever danced before. Sensing that lying was useless, I told her my dancing lesson story. Instead of asking me to take her home, she laughed and said that she would be just as happy if we went for a nice dinner. As we were walking toward the exit, she stopped, looked me straight in the eye and said, "Promise me that you'll never take me dancing again!" We continued to see each other, and I never did.

⁓

I arrived home from work one day to find a letter from the Canadian consulate waiting for me. I ripped it open but it was unfortunately written in English, a language that I couldn't yet read. After several telephone calls, I managed to get the telephone number of a possible translator, and when I finally heard the contents of the letter in Polish, I was crestfallen. In cold, official-sounding language, I was informed that my medical examination had shown unexplained swollen glands in my neck and that, as a consequence, I could not immigrate to Canada for the time being. The swollen glands might indicate tuber-culosis, which was highly contagious. The next paragraph stated that I would be put under a few months of observation, that the Canadian authorities believed that better nourishment and living conditions would improve my health and eventually allow them to issue me a Canadian immigration visa.

Józiek, Ronia, Maurice, Morisette and Henri went out of their way to encourage me to change my diet, stop smoking and get more sleep instead of pursuing my nocturnal adventures. They were sure that if I followed all their advice, I would soon be admitted to Canada. With a new resolve to change my life, I continued working and enjoying myself despite the difficult economic situation for most Parisians. Some foods such as sugar, meat, butter and other milk products were still rationed. I even learned to eat horse meat like a good Parisian, though I found it hard to overcome my initial squeamishness.

While I was waiting to re-apply for Canadian immigration, I came home from work to find a letter from an Austrian acquaintance of my father's younger brother Stach who had survived the war in Bucharest and fled Romania, now under Communist rule, to Vienna, where he was now living with his gentile wife. I later found out that Stach tried to immigrate to Canada, but for some unknown reason was not permitted to and died a few years later. The letter said that Uncle Stach had given him a large sum of money for me. I was to call and arrange a meeting with him, so that he could give me the money and tell me more about my uncle.

A few days later, I entered the impressive lobby of the King George Hotel and asked for the room number of my uncle's acquaintance. Our meeting didn't last long since we had no common language except broken French but what I was able to understand was that Uncle Stach was well, married without children and had been very happy to learn of my miraculous survival. The acquaintance said that my uncle would like to see me, that he missed terribly the members of the family who had been killed in the Holocaust. The messenger then repeated that he had a large sum of money to give me. I don't remember the exact amount, but I do remember that it was in American dollars, which I subsequently exchanged on the black market for francs as I needed them. On the way home from the hotel, I remember planning what I would buy with it. First on my list was a fashionable Humphrey Bogart–style raincoat complete with a belt and epaulettes.

In November 1947, the United Nations voted in favour of creating a Jewish state in Palestine and on May 14, 1948, the creation of the

State of Israel was proclaimed, just before the British mandate over Palestine ended. Parisians were divided as to whether a Jewish state should be created, but the divisions were not strictly along religious or ethnic lines. On the long-awaited day, everybody crowded around their radios and the atmosphere was thick with tension. Even the Parisian taxi drivers, famous for their constant, unnecessary honking, showed respect for the solemnity of the historic moment by driving silently.

When the news broke, pandemonium spread through the streets. In the Jewish quarter close to my hotel, strangers hugged each other and religious Jews prayed aloud on the street or danced with each other. In the next few days, in newspapers and pamphlets and on placards, Jewish organizations prepared people for the rapid mobilization of any able-bodied person willing to go to Israel. With lightning speed, demonstrations, parades and speeches took place all over Paris in the largest auditoriums and in outdoor public places. I attended some of them and remember that the audiences were not just Jewish. I heard many different European languages spoken and remember one incident in particular: I was speaking Polish with a group of friends when several Polish men approached us and declared that they would like to volunteer to go to Israel. When we asked them why, they said that they wanted to help Jewish people fight anyone who attacked them since they knew that many Jews had fought with the Soviet army to expel the Germans from Poland.

The would-be Polish volunteers moved away from my group and a small orchestra began to play. Although they were dressed in civilian clothes, they played a military march. If memory serves me right, it was a patriotic Jewish melody. People stood up and threw their hats in the air. They were weeping, hugging and kissing. The marchers came into the rear of the hall in columns carrying flags with the blue Star of David on a white background, soon to become the official flag of Israel. Representatives of other countries also carried their respective flags.

Among the Jewish groups were banners representing different political and military organizations, such as the Haganah, Irgun and Stern. At the sight of these banners, the audience clapped and shouted as loudly as they could. Finally, the organizers succeeded in silencing the crowd. The master of ceremonies announced in French and Yiddish that the official meeting would begin with the singing of "Hatikvah," the unofficial national anthem of the Jews even in exile, long before the State of Israel was established. It was a moment that I will never forget, the image of which was burned in my mind forever.

It was only when I got back to my hotel that I started to reflect on the afternoon. I had doubts about immigrating to Canada, which was a new feeling generated by the strong emotions created by the day's events. I compared myself to Piotr Ruff, whom I had last seen at the Château de Montintin. I felt that he had a noble goal and I believed that he would pursue it to the end. In my case, it seemed I had too many irons in the fire, but no goals that I could be sure of achieving. In his letters to me, Piotr described his excitement at the prospect of going to Israel. On one hand, the prospect of immigrating to Canada under the sponsorship of a powerful, influential family and of an al-most guaranteed, trouble-free and comfortable future had a powerful attraction for me. On the other hand, joining the many volunteers going to defend Israel and fight in the newly created Israeli army was a romantic idea and an answer to the call of duty.

During the next few weeks, my every free moment was spent visiting newly opened Jewish information centres with my group of friends. In reality, visiting such centres represented the first step to-ward enrolling as a volunteer in the Israeli army. Not a day passed that one of the members of my group didn't leave France for Israel.

The news coming from Israel was, in fact, alarming as the new state was attacked by its Arab neighbours. I thought about my short military career in the 1944 Warsaw Uprising. My participation in that revolt had been a rewarding experience – above all it was a way for me to take revenge for the mass murder of the Jews. I had also felt very patriotic and saw myself as answering the call of duty. If I went to Israel, I would be fighting to ensure that Jewish people could live in security in their own country. Surely it would be a nobler deed than fighting in the uprising, all the more so because I had such mixed feelings about Poland and Poles, which remained with me for many years. As I grew older, however, I realized that it was unjust to condemn a whole nation on the basis of the behaviour of a few. This partial reconciliation of my feelings allowed me, much later, to return twice to Poland with my wife, and visit the Poles who had been kind to me and had even helped save my life while risking their own.

I shared my indecision with my relatives and friends. I don't know what finally made me decide, but one morning I went to the factory and announced to Maurice and Henri that, after great deliberation and listening to many different opinions, including theirs, I had decided to go to Israel. Henri, being more pragmatic, gave me a serious look, closed the door to the outer hall and whispered that he had a rifle that he had taken from a German soldier. He said he would give it to me to take to Israel. Maurice suggested that I go to the flea market and buy an appropriate military uniform, boots and a knapsack, taking into account the hot climate in Israel, adding, "I'll pay for all this, of course, but bring me the receipt." I left the factory feeling a foot taller.

The next thing to do was to inform Ronia and Józiek of my decision. Ronia told me that I had had enough of the hard life and of living with death all around me and deserved to take advantage of the opportunity given to me by our relatives in Canada. Józiek, on the other hand, reminded me that he had left his father's house at the same age as I was now, had managed to live alone, to earn his own living and to survive without anyone's help. His view was that by going to Israel, I could serve my country and live, dangerously but honourably, in a land that would adopt me.

I still felt no more resolute than before. Thinking back now, I see that an important basis for my decision to go to Israel – in addition to the effect of that amazing experience on May 14 – was that I had received no assurance as to when, or even if, I would be given a visa for Canada. Feeling very positive, patriotic and a bit romantic, I announced to everyone my irrevocable decision to go to Israel, to take up arms and fight for our country.

I spent the next few days visiting my relatives and friends and then went to the headquarters of the organization responsible for transporting volunteers to Israel, where I received the date and time for my departure by train from Gare Saint-Lazare to Marseille. That still gave me a few days to spend with Józiek and Ronia. On the morning of my departure, I put on my new military outfit, grabbed my knapsack, called a taxi and, with some anxiety, gave the driver my destination.

Our train was already waiting on the platform when I arrived and was slowly filling with volunteers. By now, I knew many of them. I chose a seat near the window and put my knapsack on the rack above me. My thoughts jumped between the past and the future. I recalled a scene in the ghetto in 1943 a few weeks before the Jewish uprising. I had stood with my grandmother in front of the building where the five of us shared a room. It was a warm spring night, but the air was filled with the stench of dead bodies and human excrement. The street was covered with clothes, broken furniture, pillows and blankets, all left by the people who had been rounded up, herded to the *Umschlagplatz*, packed into freight trains and transported to their places of execution. We stood there without speaking, yet our minds and feelings were somehow united.

Then my grandmother said something that has stayed with me all my life. "If every Jew threw one brick at the Germans, we could kill them all." I had agreed enthusiastically, thinking that this might indeed be a solution to our desperate plight. Then she turned toward me and, in a sombre tone, predicted, "One day, you will go to Palestine and become a general in the Jewish army."

The sharp sound of a whistle and orders in French and Yiddish to board the train and shut the doors wrenched me back to reality. I stood at the window, looking out at nothing in particular, when I saw Aunt Ronia waving a paper in her hand, arguing with the guard at the gate to our platform. I jumped down from the train and ran toward her. Terribly out of breath and still madly waving the paper she gasped, "Arturze! This is your permission to immigrate to Canada!"

The scene had attracted attention from other members of our organization and since my aunt spoke Yiddish, she explained what had happened. The commotion had attracted the attention of the commander of this unit of future soldiers and I asked his advice. Sounding like the military man that he was he said, "You can always go from Canada to Palestine, but I'm not so sure you could go from Palestine to Canada." I grabbed my knapsack, rejoined my aunt and within a few weeks, I set sail for Canada.

Glossary

antisemitism Prejudice, discrimination, persecution and/or hatred against Jewish people, institutions, culture and symbols.

Armia Krajowa (Polish; in English, Home Army) Also known as AK. Formed in February 1942, the Armia Krajowa was the largest Polish resistance movement in German-occupied Poland during World War II, best known for orchestrating the 1944 Warsaw Uprising. Although the organization has been criticized for antisemitism and some factions were even guilty of killing Jews, it is also true that the AK established a Section for Jewish Affairs that collected information about what was happening to Jews in Poland, centralized contacts between Polish and Jewish military organizations, and supported the Relief Council for Jews in Poland. Members of the AK also assisted Jews during the Warsaw Ghetto Uprising in 1943, both outside the ghetto walls and by joining Jewish fighters inside the ghetto. Between 1942 and 1945, hundreds of Jews joined the AK. *See also* Warsaw Uprising.

Aryan A nineteenth-century anthropological term originally used to refer to the Indo-European family of languages and, by extension, the peoples who spoke them. The term became a synonym for people of Nordic or Germanic descent in the theories that inspired Nazi racial ideology. "Aryan" was an official classification in Nazi racial laws to denote someone of pure Germanic blood, as opposed to "non-Aryans," such as Slavs, Jews, part-Jews, Roma and Sinti, and others of supposedly inferior racial stock.

Battle of Britain The German effort to incapacitate the Royal Air Force (RAF) by both bombing airfields and waging air battles, and the successful British defence from July through September 1940. The RAF's defence was comprised of close to 2,400 British pilots and 575 pilots from other countries; approximately 150 were from Poland.

breviary A liturgical book comprised of Catholic prayers, hymns and psalms.

British Broadcasting Corporation (BBC) The British public service broadcaster. During World War II, the BBC broadcast radio programming to Europe in German and the languages of the occupied countries. Allied forces used some of this programming to send coded messages to resistance groups. It was illegal to listen to these broadcasts, but many people in Nazi-occupied Europe turned to it as the most reliable source of news.

British Mandate Palestine The area of the Middle East under British rule from 1923 to 1948, as established by the League of Nations after World War I. During that time, the United Kingdom severely restricted Jewish immigration. The Mandate area encompassed present-day Israel, Jordan, the West Bank and the Gaza Strip.

catechism A reference text and guide to the Catholic religion in a question-and-answer format to help teach the doctrine of the faith.

challah (Hebrew) Braided egg bread traditionally eaten on the Jewish Sabbath, Shabbat, as well as on other Jewish holidays.

chazzan (Hebrew; in English, cantor) A person who leads a Jewish congregation in prayer. The cantor is usually professionally trained in music because it plays such a large role in Jewish religious services.

circumcision Removal of the foreskin of the penis. In Judaism, ritual circumcision is performed on the eighth day of a male infant's life in a religious ceremony known as a *brit milah* (Hebrew) or *bris* (Yiddish) to welcome him into the covenant between God and the People of Israel.

Geneva Conventions A set of treaties and protocols that were negotiated between 1864 and 1949 to establish an international law for the standards of humanitarian treatment of victims of war, both military and civilian.

Gestapo (German; abbreviation of Geheime Staatspolizei, the Secret State Police of Nazi Germany) The Gestapo was the brutal force that dealt with the perceived enemies of the Nazi regime and was responsible for rounding up European Jews for deportation to the death camps. They operated with very few legal constraints and were also responsible for issuing exit visas to the residents of German-occupied areas. A number of Gestapo members also joined the Einsatzgruppen, the mobile killing squads responsible for the roundup and murder of Jews in eastern Poland and the USSR through mass shooting operations.

ghetto A confined residential area for Jews. The term originated in Venice, Italy in 1516 with a law requiring all Jews to live on a segregated, gated island known as Ghetto Nuovo. Throughout the Middle Ages in Europe, Jews were often forcibly confined to gated Jewish neighbourhoods. During the Holocaust, the Nazis forced Jews to live in crowded and unsanitary conditions in run-down districts of cities and towns; in Poland, most ghettos were enclosed by brick walls or wooden fences with barbed wire. The Warsaw ghetto was the largest in Poland, with more than 400,000 crowded into an area of just over 300 hectares; the Lodz ghetto, with more than 160,000, was the second largest. *See also* Warsaw ghetto.

Haganah (Hebrew; The Defense) The Jewish paramilitary force in British Mandate Palestine that existed from 1920 to 1948 and later became the Israel Defense Forces. After World War II, there were branches of the Haganah in the DP camps in Europe, and members helped coordinate illegal immigration to British Mandate Palestine. *See also* Irgun.

Hatikvah (Hebrew; literally, the hope) A poem composed by Naphtali Herz Imber in 1878 that was set to a folk melody and adopted by early Zionist groups in Europe as their anthem, including the First Zionist Congress in 1897. When the State of Israel was established in 1948, it was unofficially proclaimed the national anthem; it officially became so in 2004.

Irgun (abbreviated from Irgun Zvai Le'umi; Hebrew; National Military Organization) The Irgun (also known as the Etzel, its Hebrew acronym) was formed in 1937, after separating from the Haganah military force. Due to the increasing level of violence between Arab and Jewish citizens, the Irgun advocated active and armed resistance, as opposed to the policy of restraint that was advocated by the Haganah. The Irgun was also fundamental to the illegal transport and immigration of thousands of European Jews into British Mandate Palestine. The activities of the Irgun were controversial – some viewed them as a terrorist organization, while others applauded their efforts as freedom fighters.

Jedna Pani Powiedziała (JPP) (Polish; in English, one woman said) An informal, local rumour network.

Jewish Council (in German, *Judenrat*) A group of Jewish leaders appointed by the Nazis to administer and provide services to the local Jewish population under occupation and carry out Nazi orders. The council, which appeared to be a self-governing entity but was actually under complete Nazi control, faced difficult and complex moral decisions under brutal conditions and remains a contentious subject. The chairmen had to decide whether to comply or refuse to comply with Nazi demands. Some were killed by the Nazis for refusing, while others committed suicide. Jewish officials who advocated compliance thought that cooperation might save at least some of the population. Some who denounced resistance efforts did so because they believed that armed resistance would bring death to the entire community.

Jewish ghetto police (in German, Ordnungsdienst; literally, Order Service) The force established by the Jewish Councils, under Nazi order, that was armed with clubs and carried out various tasks in the ghettos, such as traffic control and guarding the ghetto gates. Eventually, some policemen also participated in rounding up Jews for forced labour and transportation to the death camps and carried out the orders of the Nazis. There has been much debate and controversy surrounding the role of both the Jewish Councils and the Jewish police. Even though the Jewish police exercised considerable power within the ghetto, to the Nazis these policemen were still Jews and subject to the same fate as other Jews.

kibbutz (Hebrew) A collectively owned farm or settlement in Israel democratically governed by its members.

Kielce pogrom The July 1946 riots in a city in Poland where about 250 Jews lived after the war (the pre-war Jewish population had been more than 20,000). After the false report of a young Polish boy kidnapped by Jews, police arrested and beat Jewish residents in the city, inciting a mob of hundreds of Polish civilians to violently attack and kill forty Jews while police stood by. Combined with other post-war antisemitic incidents throughout Poland – other pogroms occurred in Rzeszów, Krakow, Tarnów and Sosnowiec, and robberies and blackmail were common – this event was the catalyst for a mass exodus; between July 1945 and September 1946, more than 80,000 Jews left Poland.

Lord's Prayer (in Latin, Oratio Dominica, also called Pater Noster, "Our Father") A common prayer in Christian liturgy, it appears in the New Testament in two versions (short and long) as part of the teachings of Jesus and as a model of prayer.

macher (Yiddish; literally, maker) A term that either refers to an important, influential person who gets things done, or, in slang, a big shot.

Nuremberg Laws The September 1935 laws that stripped Jews of their civil rights as German citizens and separated them from Germans legally, socially and politically. They were first announced at the Nazi party rally in the city of Nuremberg in 1933. Under "The Law for the Protection of German Blood and Honour" Jews were defined as a separate race rather than a religious group; whether a person was racially Jewish was determined by ancestry (how many Jewish grandparents a person had). Among other things, the law forbade marriages or sexual relations between Jews and Germans.

OSE (Œuvre de Secours aux Enfants) (French; Children's Relief Agency) A French-Jewish organization that helped rescue thousands of Jewish refugee children during World War II. The OSE was founded in Russia in 1912 and relocated its offices to France in 1933, where it set up more than a dozen orphanages and homes; hid children from the Nazis; and, among other underground operations, arranged for their transfer to the US and Switzerland.

partisans Members of irregular military forces or resistance movements formed to oppose armies of occupation. During World War II there were a number of different partisan groups that opposed both the Nazis and their collaborators in several countries. The term partisan could include highly organized, almost paramilitary groups such as the Red Army partisans; ad hoc groups bent more on survival than resistance; and roving groups of bandits who plundered what they could from all sides during the war. In Poland, the partisans were collectively known as the Polish Underground State and the primary armed partisan group developed into the Armia Krajowa, the Polish Home Army. There were several Polish resistance movements, often fiercely opposed to one another on ideological grounds, and at least one, the National Armed Forces, was violently antisemitic. *See also* Armia Krajowa.

Passover One of the major festivals of the Jewish calendar, Passover takes place over eight days in the spring. One of the main observances of the holiday is to recount the story of Exodus, the Jews' flight from slavery in Egypt, at a ritual meal called a seder. The name itself refers to the fact that God "passed over" the houses of the Jews when he set about slaying the first-born sons of Egypt as the last of the ten plagues aimed at convincing Pharaoh to free the Jews.

Pawiak prison A facility built in Warsaw in 1835 between Dzielna, Pawia and Wiezlenna streets, which later became part of the Warsaw ghetto. Between October 1939 and August 1944, the Gestapo and the SD – the German security police – controlled the prison and the more than 65,000 prisoners who passed through it, subjecting them to horrendous conditions, interrogations, executions and deportations to Nazi camps. The majority of inmates were Polish political prisoners from Warsaw, though the prison also held Jews caught outside the ghetto and Soviet prisoners of war. German officers blew up Pawiak prison on August 21, 1944.

Polska Partia Robotnicza (PPR) (Polish; in English, Polish Workers' Party) A communist organization created in 1942 that was affiliated with the Soviet Communist Party. The PPR established the Armia Ludowa (People's Army), a communist partisan force, to support Soviet military action against the Nazis; the party also supported a future communist-led government in Poland.

Rada Główna Opiekuńcza (RGO) (Polish; in English, Central Welfare Council) A welfare organization that provided social services to children, the poor and the displaced during both World War I and II. The RGO was sanctioned by the German occupation and also had ties to the Polish underground.

Red Cross A humanitarian organization founded in 1863 to protect the victims of war. During WWII the Red Cross provided assistance to prisoners of war by distributing food parcels and monitoring the situation in POW camps, and also provided medical attention to wounded soldiers and civilians. Today, in addition to the international body, there are National Red Cross and Red Crescent societies in almost every country in the world.

Salesian order (also known as Salesians of Don Bosco) A Roman Catholic society founded by Saint John Bosco in the late nineteenth century. The society, which continues to operate today with more than 20,000 members, focuses on charitable works to children in need, operating homeless shelters and providing both religious and vocational education.

SS (German; abbreviation of Schutzstaffel, Defence Corps) The SS was established in 1925 as Adolf Hitler's elite corps of personal bodyguards. Under the direction of Heinrich Himmler, its membership grew from 280 in 1929 to 50,000 when the Nazis came to power in 1933, and to nearly a quarter of a million on the eve of World War II. The SS was comprised of the Allgemeine-SS (General SS) and the Waffen-SS (Armed, or Combat SS). The General SS dealt with policing and the enforcement of Nazi racial policies in Germany and the Nazi-occupied countries. An important unit within the SS was the Reichssicherheitshauptamt (RSHA, the Central Office of Reich Security), whose responsibility included the Gestapo (Geheime Staatspolizei). The SS ran the concentration and death camps, with all their associated economic enterprises, and also fielded its own Waffen-SS military divisions, including some recruited from the occupied countries. *See also* Gestapo.

Star of David (in Hebrew, *Magen David*) The six-pointed star that is the ancient and most recognizable symbol of Judaism. During World War II, Jews in Nazi-occupied areas were frequently forced to wear a badge or armband with the Star of David on it as an identifying mark of their lesser status and to single them out as targets for persecution.

Stern Gang The British name for the radical Jewish paramilitary and Zionist group in British Mandate Palestine that was called Lehi and led by Avraham Stern (in Hebrew, *Lohamei Herut Israel*, meaning Fighters for the Freedom of Israel). Lehi, which advocated for a Jewish state and open immigration for European Jewish refugees, split from the military organization Irgun in 1940 due to disagreement over armed conflict against the British, which Lehi supported and enacted. *See also* British Mandate Palestine; Irgun.

Treaty of Non-Aggression between Germany and the USSR The treaty that was signed on August 24, 1939, and was colloquially known as the Molotov-Ribbentrop pact, after signatories Soviet foreign minister Vyacheslav Molotov and German foreign minister Joachim von Ribbentrop. The main provisions of the pact stipulated that the two countries would not go to war with each other and that they would both remain neutral if either one was attacked by a third party. One of the key components of the treaty was the division of various independent countries – including Poland – into Nazi and Soviet spheres of influence and areas of occupation. The Nazis breached the pact by launching a major offensive against the Soviet Union on June 22, 1941.

Treblinka A labour and death camp created as part of Operation Reinhard, the German code word for the Nazi plan for murdering Jews in German-occupied Poland using poison gas. A slave-labour camp (Treblinka I) was built in November 1941 in the *Generalgouvernement* near the villages of Treblinka and Małkinia Górna, about 80 kilometres northeast of Warsaw. Treblinka II, the killing centre, was constructed in a sparsely populated and heavily wooded area about 1.5 kilometres from the labour camp in 1942 and the first massive deportations there from Warsaw began on July 22, 1942. The people who arrived in the deportations to Treblinka II were separated by sex, stripped of their clothing and other possessions, marched into buildings that they were told contained bathhouses and gassed with carbon monoxide. From July 1942 to October 1943 more than 750,000 Jews were killed at Treblinka, making it second only to Auschwitz in the numbers of Jews killed. Treblinka I and II were both liberated by the Soviet army in July 1944.

Umschlagplatz (German; collection place) The area in the Warsaw ghetto connected to a freight train station, where Jews were assembled for deportation. A memorial was built on the site in 1988.

Volksdeutsche The term used by the Nazis to refer to the ethnic Germans living outside Germany in Central and Eastern Europe. Prior to World War II, there were more than ten million ethnic Germans living in these countries, some of whose families had been there for centuries. When the Nazis occupied these territories, they intended to reclaim the *Volksdeutsche* as Germans and strengthen their communities as a central part of creating the Nazis' ideal of a Greater Germany. Ethnic Germans were often given the choice either to sign the *Volksliste*, the list of German people, and be regarded as traitors by their home countries, or not to sign and be treated as traitors to the "Germanic race" by the Nazi occupiers. After the collapse of Nazi Germany most *Volksdeutsche* were persecuted by the post-war authorities in their home countries.

Warsaw ghetto An area designated by the Germans in October 1940 that approximately 400,000 Jews were forced to relocate to. The ghetto, enclosed by a ten-foot wall, had horrific conditions – between 1940 and mid-1942, more than 83,000 people died of starvation and disease. Mass deportations to the Treblinka death camp were carried out between July and September 1942. *See also* Treblinka; *Umschlagplatz*.

Warsaw Ghetto Uprising The largest rebellion by Jews during the Holocaust, the Warsaw Ghetto Uprising developed in response to the *Gross-Aktion* – the Nazis' deportation of more than 275,000 ghetto inhabitants to slave-labour and death camps and the murder of another 30,000 of them between July and September 1942. When the Nazis initiated the dissolution of the ghetto on April 19, 1943, aiming to deport all those remaining to the Treblinka death camp, about 750 organized ghetto fighters launched an insurrection. Despite some support from Jewish and Polish resistance organizations outside the ghetto, the resistance fighters were defeated on May 16, 1943. More than 56,000 Jews were captured; about

7,000 were shot and the remainder were deported to death camps and concentration camps.

Warsaw Uprising An uprising organized by the Polish Home Army (AK) to liberate Warsaw from German occupation and initiate the establishment of an independent Poland in the post-war period. In August 1944, as the Soviet Red Army neared Praga, a suburb of Warsaw situated on the east bank of the Vistula River, the uprising began. The AK, however, had only 2,500 weapons for its 40,000 troops and the Soviets, under Joseph Stalin's orders, did not give support to the uprising. By October 2, 1944, the attempt at liberation had been crushed and the results were devastating – more than 150,000 civilians had been killed and more than 25 per cent of Warsaw had been destroyed. *See also* Armia Krajowa.

Wehrmacht (German) The German army during the Third Reich.

Yiddish A language derived from Middle High German with elements of Hebrew, Aramaic, Romance and Slavic languages, and written in Hebrew characters. Spoken by Jews in east-central Europe for roughly a thousand years from the tenth century to the mid-twentieth century, it was still the most common language among European Jews until the outbreak of World War II. There are similarities between Yiddish and contemporary German.

Yom Kippur (Hebrew; literally, day of atonement) A solemn day of fasting and repentance that comes eight days after Rosh Hashanah, the Jewish New Year, and marks the end of the high holidays.

Zionism A movement promoted by the Viennese Jewish journalist Theodor Herzl, who argued in his 1896 book *Der Judenstaat* (The Jewish State) that the best way to resolve the problem of antisemitism and persecution of Jews in Europe was to create an independent Jewish state in the historic Jewish homeland of Biblical Israel. Zionists also promoted the revival of Hebrew as a Jewish national language.

Photographs

1 Arthur's mother, Pola Ney-Holcman, holding newborn Arthur. Warsaw, 1930.
2 Jerzy Ney, Arthur's father.
3 The Ney family in wintery Warsaw. Left to right: Pola Ney-Holcman, Arthur and
   Jerzy Ney; standing in front: Arthur's sister, Eugenia. Poland, 1932.
4 Arthur and Eugenia, Poland, c. 1933.

1

2

3

1 Arthur's parents, Pola and Jerzy Ney.
2 Fourteen-year-old Eugenia in Warsaw in 1939, just before the war.
3 Arthur (in front) with his family. Left to right: Jerzy Ney, Eugenia, Pola Ney-
    Holcman and Arthur's paternal grandmother, Henia Ney. Poland, 1936.

1 Arthur at the Eiffel Tower with his aunt Ronia (centre) and uncle Józiek after the war. Paris, 1947.

2 Summer vacation with friends at YMCA Camp Otoreke in the Laurentians. Arthur is in front, centre. Ste. Adolphe de Howard, Quebec, c. 1950.

3 Arthur (left) with his cousin Benjamin Roskies, whose family sponsored Arthur's immigration to Canada. Montreal, 1952.

1 Arthur's first wife, Susan, with their son Stephen. Montreal, 1957.
2 Arthur with one-year-old son David (left) and five-year-old Stephen.

1   Arthur's reunion with Franciszek Puchała, the farmer who sheltered Arthur in Runów in 1943. Poland, 1988.

2   Arthur's reunion with Father Ignaczewski, the rector of the Salesian orphanage that gave Arthur a home in 1945. Szczaki, 1988.

3   Arthur back in Warsaw in 1988.

Arthur with students at the Montreal Holocaust Memorial Museum, 2012.

Index

The Azrieli Foundation

The The Azrieli Foundation was established in 1989 to realize and extend the philanthropic vision of David J. Azrieli, C.M., C.Q., M.Arch. The Foundation's mission is to support a wide spectrum of initiatives in education and research. The Azrieli Foundation is an active supporter of programs in the fields of Education, the education of architects, scientific and medical research, and the arts. The Azrieli Foundation's many initiatives include: the Holocaust Survivor Memoirs Program, which collects, preserves, publishes and distributes the written memoirs of survivors in Canada; the Azrieli Institute for Educational Empowerment, an innovative program successfully working to keep at-risk youth in school; the Azrieli Fellows Program, which promotes academic excellence and leadership on the graduate level at Israeli universities; the Azrieli Music Project, which celebrates and fosters the creation of high-quality new Jewish orchestral music; and the Azrieli Neurodevelopmental Research Program, which supports advanced research on neurodevelopmental disorders, particularly Fragile X and Autism Spectrum Disorders.